SCHAUM'S *Easy* OUTLINES

ELECTRONIC DEVICES

AND CIRCUITS

Other Books in Schaum's Easy Outline Series Include:

SCHAUM'S *Easy* OUTLINES

ELECTRONIC DEVICES

AND CIRCUITS

BASED ON SCHAUM'S
Outline of Theory and Problems of
Electronic Devices and Circuits

BY

JIMMIE J. CATHEY, Ph.D.

ABRIDGEMENT EDITOR:
WILLIAM T. SMITH, Ph.D.

SCHAUM'S OUTLINE SERIES

McGRAW-HILL

New York   Chicago   San Francisco   Lisbon   London   Madrid   Mexico City
Milan   New Delhi   San Juan   Seoul   Singapore   Sydney   Toronto

1 2 3 4 5 6 7 8 9 DOC/DOC 0 9 8 7 6 5

ISBN 0-07-145532-9

JIMMIE J. CATHEY earned the Ph.D. from Texas A&M University and has 13 years of industrial experience in the design and development of electric device systems. Since 1980, he has taught at the University of Kentucky. His research and teaching interests are power electronics, electric machines, and robotics. He is a Registered Professional Engineer.

WILLIAM T. SMITH is Associate Professor in the department of electrical engineering at the University of Kentucky, where he has taught since 1990 and has twice won the Outstanding Engineering Professor Award. He earned a B.S. degree from the University of Kentucky and both M.S. and Ph.D. degrees in electrical engineering from the Virginia Polytechnic Institute and State University. He was an academic visitor at the IBM Austin Research Laboratory and previously worked as a senior engineer in the Government Aerospace Systems Division of Harris Corporation. He is also the co-author of several journal articles and conference papers and served as abridgment editor of *Schaum's Easy Outline: Basic Electricity*, *Schaum's Easy Outline: Electromagnetics*, and *Schaum's Easy Outline: Electric Circuits*.

Contents

Chapter 1
CIRCUIT ANALYSIS: PORT POINT OF VIEW

IN THIS CHAPTER:

- ✔ *Circuit Elements*
- ✔ *Circuit Laws*
- ✔ *Network Theorems*
- ✔ *Two-Port Networks*
- ✔ *Instantaneous, Average, and RMS Values*

Circuit Elements

Electronic devices are described by their nonlinear terminal voltage-current characteristics. Circuits containing electronic devices are analyzed and designed either by utilizing graphs of experimentally measured characteristics or by linearizing the voltage-current characteristics of the devices. Depending on applicability, the latter approach involves

1

2 ELECTRONIC DEVICES AND CIRCUITS

the formulation of either small-perturbation equations valid about an operating point or a piecewise-linear equation set. The linearized equation set describes the circuit in terms of its interconnected passive elements and independent or controlled voltage and current sources whose formulation and solution require knowledge of the circuit analysis and circuit reduction principles reviewed in this chapter.

The time-stationary (or constant value) elements of Fig. 1-1(a) to (c) (the resistor, inductor, and capacitor, respectively) are called *passive elements* since none of them can continuously supply energy to a circuit. For voltage v and current i, we have the following relationships: For the resistor,

$$v = Ri \text{ or } i = Gv \tag{1.1}$$

where R is its *resistance* in ohms (Ω) and $G = 1/R$ is its *conductance* in siemens (S).

Note!

Equation (1.1) is known as *Ohm's Law.*

For the inductor,

$$v = L\frac{di}{dt} \quad \text{or} \quad i = \frac{1}{L} \int_{-\infty}^{t} v\,d\tau \tag{1.2}$$

where L is its *inductance* in henrys (H). For the capacitor,

$$v = \frac{1}{C} \int_{-\infty}^{t} i\,d\tau \quad \text{or} \quad i = C\frac{dv}{dt} \tag{1.3}$$

where C is the capacitance in farads (F).

If R, L, and C are independent of voltage and current (as well as of time), these elements are said to be *linear*.

The elements of Fig. 1-1(d) to (h) are called *active elements*. Each is capable of continuously supplying energy to a network. The *ideal volt-*

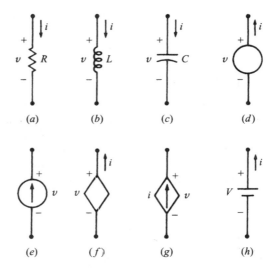

Fig. 1-1 Circuit element symbols

age source in Fig. 1-1(*d*) provides a terminal voltage *v* that is independent of the current *i* flowing through it. The *ideal current source* in Fig. 1.1(*e*) provides a current *i* that is independent of the voltage *v* across its terminals. However, the *controlled* (or *dependent*) *voltage source* in Fig. 1-1(*f*) has a terminal voltage that depends on the voltage across or current through some other element of the network. Similarly, the *controlled* (or *dependent*) *current source* in Fig. 1-1(*g*) provides a current whose magnitude depends on either the voltage across or current through some other element of the network.

Remember

If the dependency relation for the voltage or current of a controlled source is of the first degree, then the source is called a *linear* controlled (or dependent) source.

The *battery* or *dc voltage source* in Fig. 1-1(*h*) is a special kind of independent voltage source.

Circuit Laws

Along with the three voltage-current relationships (1.1) to (1.3), Kirchhoff's laws are sufficient to formulate the simultaneous equations necesary to solve for all currents and voltages of a network (the term *network* is used to denote any arrangement of circuit elements).

Kirchhoff's voltage law (KVL) states that the algebraic sum of all voltages around any closed loop of a circuit is zero:

$$\sum_{k=1}^{n} v_k = 0$$

where *n* is the number of passive- and active-element voltages around the loop under consideration.

Kirchhoff's current law states that the algebraic sum of all currents entering a node must be zero:

$$\sum_{k=1}^{m} i_k = 0$$

where *m* is the total number of currents flowing into the node under consideration.

At some (sufficiently long) time after a circuit containing linear elements is energized, the voltages and currents become independent of initial conditions and the time variation of circuit quantities and currents become identical to that of the independent sources. The circuit is said to be operating in the *steady state*. On the other hand, if the magnitude of each nondependent source can be written as $K \sin(\omega t + \phi)$ where K is a constant, then the resulting steady state is known as *sinusoidal steady state* and well-known frequency domain, or phasor, methods are applicable in its analysis. In general, electronic circuit analysis is a combination of dc and sinusoidal steady-state analysis using the principle of *superposition* (see the next section).

Network Theorems

A *linear network* (or *linear circuit*) is formed by interconnecting the terminals of independent sources, linear controlled sources, and linear passive elements to form one or more closed paths. The *superposition theorem* states that in a linear network containing multiple sources, the voltage across or current through any passive element may be found as the algebraic sum of the individual voltages or currents due to each of the *independent* sources acting alone, with all other sources deactivated.

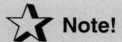 **Note!**

An ideal voltage source is deactivated by replacing it with a short circuit. An ideal current source is deactivated by replacing it with an open circuit. In general, controlled sources remain active when the superposition theorem is applied.

Example 1.1 For the circuit of Fig. 1-2, $v_s = 10\sin\omega t$ V, $V_b = 10$ V, $R_1 = R_2 = R_3 = 1\Omega$ and $\alpha = 0$. Find current i_2 by use of the superposition theorem.

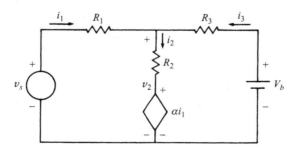

Fig. 1-2 Linear circuit example

Solution: We first deactivate V_b by shorting and use a single prime to denote a response due to V_s alone. Using the method of node voltages with unknown v_2' and summing currents at the upper node, we have

$$\frac{v_s - v_2'}{R_1} = \frac{v_2'}{R_2} + \frac{v_2'}{R_3}$$

Substituting given values and solving for v_2' we obtain

$$v_2' = \frac{1}{3} v_s = \frac{10}{3} \sin \omega t$$

Then, by Ohm's law,

$$i_2' = \frac{v_2'}{R_2} = \frac{10}{3} \sin \omega t \ \text{A}$$

Now, deactivating vs and using a double prime to denote a response due to V_b alone, we have

$$i_3'' = \frac{V_b}{R_3 + R_1 \parallel R_2}$$

where

$$R_1 \parallel R_2 = \frac{R_1 R_2}{R_1 + R_2}$$

so that

$$i_3'' = \frac{10}{1 + 1/2} = \frac{20}{3} \ \text{A}$$

Then, by current division,

$$i_2'' = \frac{R_1}{R_1 + R_2} i_3'' = \frac{1}{2} i_3'' = \frac{10}{3} \ \text{A}$$

Finally, by the superposition theorem,

$$i_2 = i_2' + i_2'' = \frac{10}{3}(1 + \sin\omega t)\text{A}$$

Terminals in a network are usually considered in pairs. A *port* is a terminal pair across which a voltage can be identified and such that the current into one terminal is the same as the current out of the other terminal. In Fig. 1-3, if $i_1 \equiv i_2$, then terminals 1 and 2 form a port. Moreover, as viewed to the left from terminals 1,2, network A is a one-port network. Likewise, viewed to the right from terminals 1,2, network B is a one-port network.

Thévenin's theorem states that an arbitrary linear, one-port network such as network A in Fig. 1-3 can be replaced at terminals 1,2 with an equivalent series-connected voltage source V_{Th} and impedance Z_{Th} ($Z_{Th} = R_{Th} + jX_{Th}$) as shown in Fig. 1-4.

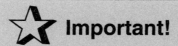 **Important!**

V_{Th} is the open-circuit voltage of network A at terminals 1, 2 with network B disconnected. Z_{Th} is the ratio of open-circuit voltage to short-circuit current of network A determined at terminals 1, 2 with network B disconnected.

If network A or B contains a controlled source, its controlling variable must be in that same network. Alternatively, Z_{Th} is the equivalent impedance looking into network A through terminals 1, 2 with all independent sources deactivated. If network A contains a controlled source, Z_{Th} is found as the *driving-point impedance* (see Example 1.2).

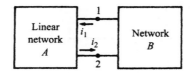

Fig. 1-3 One-port networks A and B

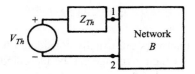

Fig. 1-4 Thévenin equivalent for network A

Example 1.2 In the circuit of Fig. 1-5, $V_A = 4$ V, $\alpha = 0.25$ A/V, $R_1 = 2\Omega$, and $R_2 = 3\Omega$. Find the Thévenin equivalent voltage and impedance for the network to the left of terminals 1, 2.

Solution: With terminals 1, 2 open-circuited, no current flows through R_2. But the control variable V_L for the voltage-controlled dependent source is still contained in the network to the left of terminals 1, 2. Application of KVL yields

$$V_{Th} = V_L = V_A + \alpha V_{Th} R_1$$

So that

$$V_{Th} = \frac{V_A}{1 - \alpha R_1} = \frac{4}{1 - (0.25)(2)} = 8 \text{ V}$$

Since the network to the left of terminals 1, 2 contains a controlled source, Z_{Th} is found as the driving-point impedance V_{dp}/I_{dp} with the network to

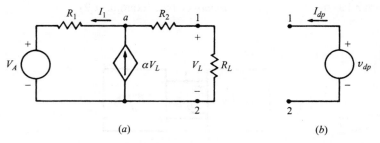

(a)   (b)

Fig. 1-5 (a) Circuit example; (b) driving point source

the right of terminals 1, 2 in Fig. 1-5(a) replaced by the driving-point source of Fig. 1-5(b) and V_A deactivated (short-circuited). After these changes, KCL applied at node a gives

$$I_1 = \alpha V_{dp} + I_{dp} \qquad (1.4)$$

Application of KVL around the outer loop of this circuit (with V_A still deactivated) yields

$$V_{dp} = I_{dp} R_2 + I_1 R_1 \qquad (1.5)$$

Substitution of (1.4) into (1.5) allows for solution for Z_{Th} as

$$Z_{Th} = \frac{V_{dp}}{I_{dp}} = \frac{R_1 + R_2}{1 - \alpha R_1} = \frac{2 + 3}{1 - (0.25)(2)} = 10\ \Omega$$

Norton's theorem states that an arbitrary linear, passive one-port network such as network A in Fig. 1-3 can be replaced at terminals 1, 2 by an equivalent parallel-connected current source I_N and admittance Y_N as shown in Fig. 1-6.

You Need to Know

I_N is the short-circuit current that flows from terminal 1 to terminal 2 due to network A and Y_N is the ratio of short circuit current to open-circuit voltage at terminals 1, 2 with network B disconnected.

If network A or B contains a controlled source, its controlling variable must be in that same network. It is apparent that $Y_N \equiv 1/Z_{Th}$. Thus, any method for determining Z_{Th} is equally valid for any finding Y_N.

Example 1.3 Find the Norton equivalent current I_N for the circuit to the left of terminals 1, 2 in Fig. 1-7. $V_A = 4$ V, $I_A = 2$ A, $R_1 = 2\Omega$, and $R_2 = 3\Omega$.

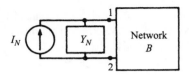

Fig. 1-6 Norton equivalent circuit for network *A*

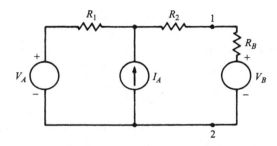

Fig. 1-7 Norton equivalent circuit example

Solution: The Norton current is found as the short-circuit current from terminal 1 to terminal 2 by superposition. It is

$$I_N = I_{12} = \text{current due to } V_A + \text{current due to } I_A$$

$$= \frac{V_A}{R_1 + R_2} + \frac{R_1 I_A}{R_1 + R_2} = \frac{4}{2+3} + \frac{(2)(2)}{2+3} = 1.6 \text{ A}$$

The Norton admittance Y_N will be found by first calculating Z_{Th}. Since there are no sources, we may find the equivalent impedance looking to the left of terminals 1, 2 by deactivating the independent sources (short-circuit for V_A and open-circuit for I_A). The Thévenin impedance is

$$Z_{Th} = R_1 + R_2 = 2 + 3 = 5\Omega$$

$$\Rightarrow Y_N = 1/Z_{Th} = 0.2 \text{ S}$$

We shall sometimes double-subscript voltages and currents to show the terminals that are of interest. Thus, V_{13} is the voltage across terminals 1 and 3, where terminal 1 is assumed at a higher potential than terminal 3. Similarly, I_{13} is the current that flows from terminal 1 to terminal 3. As an example, V_L in Fig. 1-5(a) could be labeled V_{12} (but not V_{21}).

Note also that an active element (either independent or controlled) is restricted to its assigned, or stated, current or voltage, no matter what is involved in the rest of the circuit. Thus, the controlled source in Fig 1-5(a) will provide αV_L A no matter what voltage is required to do so and no matter what changes take place in other parts of the circuit.

Two-Port Networks

The network of Fig. 1-8 is a *two-port network* if $I_1 = I_1'$ and $I_2 = I_2'$. It can be characterized by the four variables V_1, V_2, I_1, and I_2, only two of which can be independent.

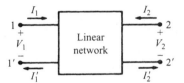

Fig. 1-8 Two-port network

If V_1 and V_2 are taken as independent variables and the linear network contains no independent sources, the independent and dependent variables are related by the z parameters.

The z parameters are the *open-circuit impedance parameters* z_{11}, z_{12}, z_{21}, and z_{22} are related through the equation set

$$V_1 = z_{11}I_1 + z_{12}I_2$$

$$V_2 = z_{21}I_1 + z_{22}I_2$$

Each of the z parameters can be evaluated by setting the proper current to zero (or, equivalently, by open-circuiting an appropriate port of the network). They are

$$z_{11} = \frac{V_1}{I_1}\bigg|_{I_2=0} \qquad z_{12} = \frac{V_1}{I_2}\bigg|_{I_1=0}$$

$$z_{21} = \frac{V_2}{I_1}\bigg|_{I_2=0} \qquad z_{22} = \frac{V_2}{I_2}\bigg|_{I_1=0}$$

(1.6)

In a similar manner, if V_1 and I_2 are taken as the independent variables, a characterization of the two-port network via the *hybrid parameters* or, simply, *h-parameters* results with

$$V_1 = h_{11}I_1 + h_{12}V_2$$

$$I_2 = h_{21}I_1 + h_{22}V_2$$

Two of the h parameters are determined by short-circuiting port 2, while the remaining two parameters are found by open-circuiting port 1:

$$h_{11} = \frac{V_1}{I_1}\bigg|_{V_2=0} \qquad h_{12} = \frac{V_1}{V_2}\bigg|_{I_1=0}$$

$$h_{21} = \frac{I_2}{I_1}\bigg|_{V_2=0} \qquad h_{22} = \frac{I_2}{V_2}\bigg|_{I_1=0}$$

(1.7)

Example 1.4 Find the z parameters for the two-port network of Fig. 1-9.

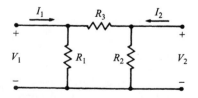

Fig. 1-9 Two-port network example

Solution: With port 2 (on the right) open-circuited, $I_2 = 0$ and the use of (1.6) gives

$$z_{11} = \frac{V_1}{I_1}\bigg|_{I_2 = 0} = R_1 \parallel (R_2 + R_3) = \frac{R_1(R_2 + R_3)}{R_1 + R_2 + R_3}$$

Also, the current I_{R2} flowing downward through R_2 is, by current division,

$$I_{R2} = \frac{R_1}{R_1 + R_2 + R_3} I_1$$

But, by Ohm's law,

$$V_2 = I_{R2} R_2 = \frac{R_1 R_2}{R_1 + R_2 + R_3} I_1$$

Hence, from (1.6)

$$z_{21} = \frac{V_2}{I_1}\bigg|_{I_2 = 0} = \frac{R_1 R_2}{R_1 + R_2 + R_3}$$

Similarly, with port 1 open-circuited, $I_1 = 0$ and (1.6) leads to

$$z_{22} = \frac{V_2}{I_2}\bigg|_{I_1 = 0} \quad R_2 \parallel (R_1 + R_3) = \frac{R_2(R_1 + R_3)}{R_1 + R_2 + R_3}$$

The use of current division to find the current downward through R_1 yields

$$I_{R1} = \frac{R_2}{R_1 + R_2 + R_3} I_2$$

And Ohm's law gives

$$V_1 = I_{R1} R_1 = \frac{R_1 R_2}{R_1 + R_2 + R_3} I_2$$

Thus,

$$z_{12} = \frac{V_1}{I_2}\bigg|_{I_1=0} = \frac{R_1 R_2}{R_1 + R_2 + R_3}$$

Example 1.5 Find the h parameters for the two-port network of Fig. 1-9.

Solution: With port 2 short-circuited, using (1.7),

$$h_{11} = \frac{V_1}{I_1}\bigg|_{V_2=0} = R_1 \parallel R_3 = \frac{R_1 R_3}{R_1 + R_3}$$

By current division,

$$I_2 = -\frac{R_1}{R_1 + R_3} I_1$$

so that, again using (1.7),

$$h_{21} = \frac{I_2}{I_1}\bigg|_{V_2=0} = -\frac{R_1}{R_1 + R_3}$$

If port 1 is open-circuited, voltage division and (1.7) lead to

$$V_1 = \frac{R_1}{R_1 + R_3} V_2$$

$$h_{12} = \frac{V_1}{V_2}\bigg|_{I_1=0} = \frac{R_1}{R_1 + R_3}$$

Finally, h_{22} is the admittance looking into port 2, as given by (1.7)

$$h_{22} = \frac{I_2}{V_2}\bigg|_{I_1=0} = \frac{1}{R_2 \parallel (R_1 + R_3)} = \frac{R_1 + R_2 + R_3}{R_2(R_1 + R_3)}$$

Instantaneous, Average, and RMS Values

The *instantaneous value* of a quantity is the value of that quantity at a specific time. Often we will be interested in the average value of a time-varying quantity. But obviously, the average of a sinusoidal function over one period is zero. For sinusoids, then, another concept, that of the *root-mean-square* (or *rms*) value, is more useful.

For any time-varying function $f(t)$ with period T, the *average value* over one period is given by

$$F_0 = \frac{1}{T} \int_{t_0}^{t_0+T} f(t)\, dt \tag{1.8}$$

and the corresponding *rms* value is defined as

$$F = \sqrt{\frac{1}{T} \int_{t_0}^{t_0+T} f^2(t)\, dt} \tag{1.9}$$

where, of course, F_0 and F are independent of t_0.

The motive for introducing rms values can be gathered from Ex. 1.6.

Example 1.6 Consider a resistance R connected directly across a dc voltage source V_{dc}. The power absorbed by R is

$$P_{dc} = \frac{V_{dc}^2}{R} \tag{1.10}$$

Now, replace V_{dc} with an ac voltage source $v(t) = V_m \sin \omega t$. The *instantaneous power* is now given by

$$p(t) = \frac{v^2(t)}{R} = \frac{V_m^2}{R} \sin^2 \omega t$$

Hence, the *average power* over one period is, by (1.8)

$$P_0 = \frac{1}{2\pi} \int_0^{2\pi} \frac{V_m^2}{R} \sin^2 \omega t \, d(\omega t) = \frac{V_m^2}{2R} \tag{1.11}$$

Comparing (1.10) and (1.11), we se that, insofar as power dissipation is concerned, an ac source of amplitude V_m is equivalent to a dc source of magnitude

$$\frac{V_m}{\sqrt{2}} = \sqrt{\frac{1}{T}\int_0^T v^2(t)\,dt} \equiv V$$

For this reason, the rms value of a sinusoid, $V = V_m/\sqrt{2}$ is also called its *effective value*.

From this point on, unless an explicit statement is made to the contrary, all currents and voltages in the frequency domain (phasors) will reflect rms rather than maximum values. Thus, the time-domain voltage $v(t) = V_m\cos(\omega t + \phi)$ will be indicated in the frequency domain as $\bar{V} = V\angle\phi$ where $V = V_m/\sqrt{2}$.

Important Things to Remember

✔ *Passive elements* do not supply energy to the circuit. They either dissipate or store energy.

✔ *Active elements* are capable of continuously supplying energy to a network.

✔ *Kirchhoff's laws* are used to formulate the network equations.

✔ *Thévenin's* and *Norton's theorems* can be used to simplify network analysis.

✔ *Two-port networks* responses can be modeled using z, h, or other parameters.

✔ The *rms* value of a quantity is its dc equivalent or *effective* value.

✔ For a sinusoidal quantity, the rms value is $1/\sqrt{2}$ of its amplitude.

Additional Solved Problems

ASP 1.1 If $R_1 = 5 \ \Omega$, $R_2 = 10 \ \Omega$, $V_S = 10$ V, and $I_S = 3$ A in the circuit of Fig.1-10, find the current i using the superposition theorem.

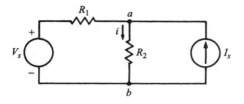

Fig. 1-10 Circuit for ASP 1.1

Solution: With I_S deactivated (open-circuited), KVL and Ohm's law give the component of i due to V_S as

$$i' = \frac{V_S}{R_1 + R_2} = \frac{10}{5 + 10} = 0.667 \text{ A}$$

With V_S deactivated (short-circuit), current division determines the component of i due to I_S:

$$i'' = \frac{R_1}{R_1 + R_2} I_S = \frac{5}{5 + 10} 3 = 1 \text{ A}$$

By superposition, the total current is

$$i = i' + i'' = 0.667 + 1 = 1.667 \text{ A}$$

ASP 1.2 For the circuit of Fig. 1-11, find v_{ab} if (a) $k = 0$ and (b) $k = 0.01$. Do not use network theorems to simplify the circuit prior to solution.

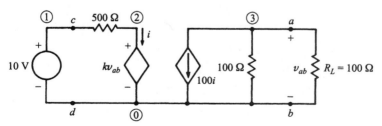

Fig. 1-11 Circuit for ASP 1.2

Solution: (*a*) For $k = 0$, the current i can be determined immediately with Ohm's law:

$$i = \frac{10}{500} = 0.02 \text{ A}$$

Since the output of the controlled current source flows through the parallel combination of two 100-Ω resistors, we have

$$v_{ab} = -(100i)(100 \parallel 100) = -100 \times 0.02 \frac{(100)(100)}{100 + 100} = -100 \text{ V} \quad \text{(A.1)}$$

(*b*) With $k \neq 0$, it is necessary to solve two simultaneous equations with unknowns i and v_{ab}. Around the left loop, KVL yields

$$0.01 v_{ab} + 500i = 10 \quad \quad \text{(A.2)}$$

With i unknown, (A.1) becomes

$$v_{ab} + 5000i = 0 \quad \quad \text{(A.3)}$$

Solving (A.2) and (A.3) simultaneously by Cramer's rule leads to

$$v_{ab} = \frac{\begin{vmatrix} 10 & 500 \\ 0 & 5000 \end{vmatrix}}{\begin{vmatrix} 0.01 & 500 \\ 1 & 5000 \end{vmatrix}} = \frac{50,000}{-450} = -111.1 \text{ V}$$

ASP 1.3 If $V_1 = 10$ V, $V_2 = 15$ V, $R_1 = 4\ \Omega$, and $R_2 = 6\ \Omega$ in the circuit of Fig. 1-12, find the Thévenin equivalent for the network to the left of terminals a,b.

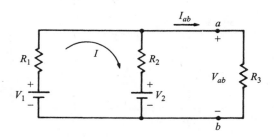

Fig. 1-12 Circuit for ASP 1.3

Solution:
With terminals a,b open-circuited, only loop current I flows. Then, by KVL,

$$V_1 - IR_1 = V_2 + IR_2$$

so that

$$I = \frac{V_1 - V_2}{R_1 + R_2} = \frac{10 - 15}{4 + 6} = -0.5 \text{ A}$$

The Thévenin equivalent voltage is then

$$V_{Th} = V_{ab} = V_1 - IR_1 = 10 - (-0.5)(4) = 12 \text{ V}$$

Deactivating (shorting) the independent voltage sources V_1 and V_2 gives the Thévenin impedance to the left of terminals a,b as

$$Z_{Th} = R_{Th} = R_1 \parallel R_2 = \frac{R_1 R_2}{R_1 + R_2} = \frac{(4)(6)}{4 + 6} = 2.4\,\Omega$$

V_{Th} and Z_{Th} are connected in as in Fig. 1-4 to produce the Thévenin equivalent circuit.

ASP 1.4 Determine the h parameters for the two-port network of Fig. 1-13.

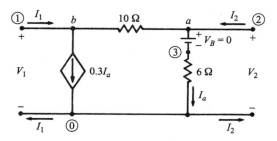

Fig. 1-13. Network for ASP 1.4

Solution: For $V_2 = 0$, $I_a = 0$. Thus, $I_1 = V_1/10$ and, by (1.7),

$$h_{11} = \left.\frac{V_1}{I_1}\right|_{V_2 = 0} = 10\,\Omega$$

Further, $I_2 = -I_1$ and, by (1.7),

$$h_{21} = \left.\frac{I_2}{I_1}\right|_{V_2=0} = -1$$

Now, $I_a = V_2/6$. With $I_1 = 0$, KVL yields

$$V_1 = V_2 - 10(0.3I_a) = V_2 - 10(0.3)\frac{V_2}{6} = 0.5V_2$$

and, from (1.7),

$$h_{12} = \left.\frac{V_1}{V_2}\right|_{I_1=0} = 0.5$$

Finally, applying KCL at node a gives

$$I_2 = I_a + 0.3I_a = 1.3\frac{V_2}{6}$$

so, that by (1.7),

$$h_{22} = \left.\frac{I_2}{V_2}\right|_{I_1=0} = \frac{1.3}{6} = 0.2167 \text{ S}$$

Chapter 2
SEMICONDUCTOR DIODES

IN THIS CHAPTER:

✔ *The Ideal Diode*
✔ *Diode Terminal Characteristics*
✔ *Graphical Analysis*
✔ *Diode Applications*
✔ *Zener Diodes*

The Ideal Diode

Diodes are among the oldest and most widely used of electronic devices. A *diode* may be defined as a near-unidirectional conductor whose state of conductivity is determined by the polarity of its terminal voltage. The subject of this chapter is the *semiconductor diode*, formed by the metallurgical junction of *p*-type and *n*-type material.

A *p*-type material is a group-IV element *doped* with a small quantity of group-V material; *n*-type material is a group-IV base element doped with a group-III material.

The symbol for the *common* or *rectifier diode* is shown in Fig. 2-1. the device has two terminals, labeled *anode* (*p*-type) and *cathode* (*n*-type), which makes understandable the choice of *diode* as its name.

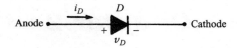

Fig. 2-1 Symbol for an ideal diode

When the terminal voltage is nonnegative ($v_D \geq 0$), the diode is said to be *forward-biased* or "on"; the positive current that flows ($i_D \geq 0$)is called *forward current*. When $v_D < 0$, the diode is said to be *reverse-biased* or "off" and the corresponding small negative current is referred to as *reverse current*.

The *ideal diode* is a perfect two-state device that exhibits zero impedance when forward-biased and infinite impedance when reverse-biased (Fig. 2-2). Since either current or voltage is zero at any instant, no power is dissipated by an ideal diode. In many circuit applications, diode forward voltage drops and reverse currents are small compared to other circuit variables; then, sufficiently accurate results are obtained if the actual diode is modeled as ideal.

The *ideal diode analysis procedure* is as follows:

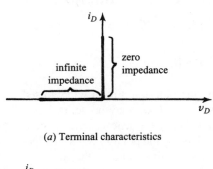

(*a*) Terminal characteristics

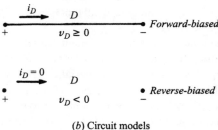

(*b*) Circuit models

Fig. 2-2 Ideal diode modeling

Step 1: Assume forward bias and replace the ideal diode with a short circuit.

Step 2: Evaluate the diode current i_D using any linear circuit-analysis technique.

Step 3: If $i_D \geq 0$, the diode is actually forward-biased, the analysis is valid and step 4 is to be omitted.

Step 4: If $i_D < 0$, the analysis so far is invalid. Replace the diode with an open circuit, forcing $i_D = 0$. Then solve for the desired circuit quantities using any method of circuit analysis. Voltage v_D must be found to have a negative value.

Example 2.1 Find voltage v_L in the circuit of Fig. 2-3, where D is an ideal diode.

Solution: The analysis is simplified if a Thévenin equivalent circuit is found for the circuit to the left of terminals a,b; the result is

$$v_{Th} = \frac{R_1}{R_1 + R_S} v_s \qquad Z_{Th} = R_{Th} = R_1 \parallel R_S = \frac{R_1 R_S}{R_1 + R_S}$$

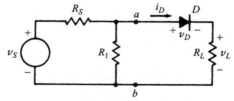

Fig. 2-3 Ideal diode example

Step 1: After replacing the network to the left of terminals a, b with the Thévenin equivalent, assume forward bias and replace diode D with a short circuit, as in Fig. 2-4(a).

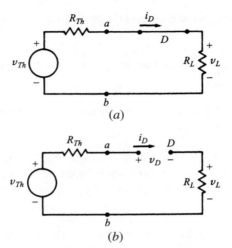

Fig. 2-4 Thévenin equivalent circuit for Ex. 2.1 solution

Step 2: By Ohm's law,

$$i_D = \frac{v_{Th}}{R_{Th} + R_L}$$

Step 3: If $v_s \geq 0$, then $i_D \geq 0$ and

$$v_L = i_D R_L = \frac{R_L}{R_{Th} + R_L} v_{Th}$$

Step 4: If $v_s < 0$, then $i_D < 0$ and the result of step 3 is invalid. Diode D must be replaced by an open circuit as illustrated in Fig. 2-4(*b*), and the analysis is performed again. Since now $i_D = 0$, $v_L = i_D R_L = 0$. Since $v_D = v_s < 0$, the reverse bias of the diode is verified.

Diode Terminal Characteristics

Use of the Fermi-Dirac probability function to predict charge neutralization gives the *static* (non-time-varying) equation for diode junction current

$$i_D = I_0(e^{v_D/\eta V_T} - 1) \text{ A} \qquad (2.1)$$

where v_D is the diode terminal voltage, $V_T \equiv kT/q$ volts, I_0 is the temperature-dependent saturation current, $k = 1.38 \times 10^{-23}$ J/K (Boltzmann's constant), $q = 1.6 \times 10^{-19}$C (electron charge) and η is an empirical constant which is 1 for germanium (Ge) and 2 for silicon (Si) diodes.

While the diode current equation serves as a useful model of the junction diode insofar as dynamic resistance is concerned, Fig. 2-5 shows it to have regions of inaccuracy:

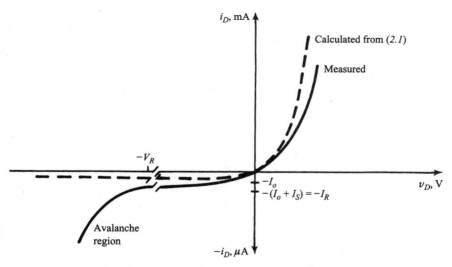

Fig. 2-5 Diode static current equation versus measured current

1. The actual (measured) forward voltage drop is greater than that predicted by (2.1) due to ohmic resistance of metal contacts and semiconductor material.
2. The actual reverse current for $-V_R \leq v_D \leq 0$ is greater than predicted due to leakage current I_S along the surface of the semiconductor material.
3. The actual reverse current increases to significantly larger values than predicted for $v_D < -V_R$ due to a complex phenomenon called avalanche breakdown.

Note!

In commercially available diodes, proper doping (impurity addition) of the base material results in distinct static terminal characteristics.

A comparison of Ge- and Si-base diode characteristics is shown in Fig. 2-6. If $-V_R \leq v_D \leq -0.1$ V, both diode types exhibit a near-constant reverse current I_R. Typically, $1\mu A < I_R < 500\ \mu A$ for Ge while $10^{-3}\mu A < I_R < 1\mu A$ for Si, for signal-level diodes (forward current ratings of less than 1 A). For a forward bias, the onset of low-resistance conduction is between 0.2 and 0.3 V for Ge, and between 0.6 and 0.7 V for Si. For both Si and Ge diodes, the saturation current I_o doubles for an increase in temperature of 10°C. In other words, the ratio of saturation current at temperature T_2 to that at temperature T_1 is

$$\frac{(I_o)_2}{(I_o)_1} = 2^{(T_2 - T_1)/10}$$

Static terminal characteristics are generally adequate for describing diode operation at low frequency. However, if high-frequency (above 100 kHz) or switching analysis is to be performed, it may be necessary to account for the small *depletion capacitance* (typically several picofarads) associated with a reverse–biased *p-n* junction. For a forward-biased *p-n* junction, a somewhat larger *diffusion capacitance* (typically several hundred picofarads) that is directly proportional to the forward current should be included in the model.

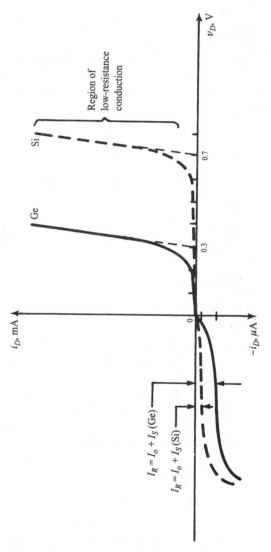

Fig. 2-6 Comparison of Ge- and Si-base diode characteristics

Graphical Analysis

A graphical solution necessarily assumes that the diode is resistive and therefore instantaneously characterized by its static i_D-versus-v_D curve. The balance of the network under study must be linear so that a Thévenin equivalent exists for it (see Fig. 2-7). Then the two simultaneous equations to be solved graphically for i_D and v_D are the diode characteristic $i_D = f_1(v_D)$ and the *load line*

$$i_D = f_2(v_D) = -\frac{1}{R_{Th}}v_D + \frac{v_{Th}}{R_{Th}} \qquad (2.2)$$

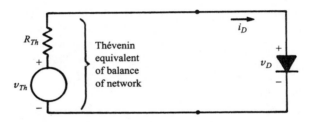

Fig. 2-7 Thévenin model required for graphical diode analysis

Example 2.2 In the circuit of Fig. 2-3, $v_s = 6$ V and $R_1 = R_S = R_L = 500\Omega$. Determine i_D and v_D graphically, using the diode characteristic in Fig. 2-8.

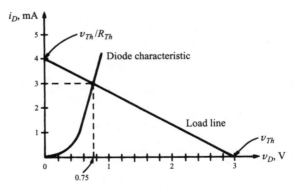

Fig. 2-8 Diode characteristic and load line for Ex. 2.2

Solution: The circuit may be reduced to that of Fig. 2-7 with

$$v_{Th} = \frac{R_1}{R_1 + R_S} v_S = \frac{500}{500 + 500} 6 = 3 \text{ V}$$

and

$$R_{Th} = R_1 \parallel R_S + R_L = \frac{(500)(500)}{500 + 500} + 500 = 750 \Omega$$

Then, with these values, the load line (2.2) must be superimposed on the diode characteristic, as in Fig. 2-8. The desired solution, $i_D = 3$ mA and $v_D = 0.75$ V, is given by the point of intersection of the two plots.

Example 2.3 If both dc and time-varying sources are present in the original linear portion of a network, then v_{Th} is a series combination of a dc and a time-varying source. Suppose that the Thévenin source for a particular network combines a 0.7-V battery and a 0.1-V-peak sinusoidal source, as in Fig. 2-9. Find i_D and v_D for the network.

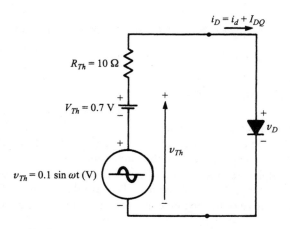

Fig. 2-9 dc/sinusoidal diode circuit example

Solution: We lay out a scaled plot of v_{Th}, with the v_{Th} axis parallel to the v_D axis of the diode characteristic curve. We then consider v_{Th}, the ac component of v_{Th} to be momentarily at zero ($t = 0$), and we plot a load line for this instant on the diode characteristic.

> ### ⭐ Important!
>
> This particular load line is called the *dc load line*, and its intersection with the diode characteristic curve is called the *quiescent point* or *Q point*.

The values of i_D and v_D at the Q point are labeled I_{DQ} and V_{DQ}, respectively, in Fig. 2-10.

In general, a number of dynamic load lines are needed to complete the analysis of i_D over a cycle of v_{Th}. However, for the network under study, only dynamic load lines for the maximum and minimum values of v_{Th} are required. The reason is that the diode characteristic is almost a straight line near the Q point (from a to b in Fig. 2-10)), so that negligible distortion if i_d, the ac component of i_D, will occur. Thus, i_d will be of the same form as v_{Th} (i.e., sinusoidal), and it can easily be sketched once the extremes of variation have been determined. The solution for i_D is thus

$$i_D = I_{DQ} + i_d = I_{DQ} + I_{dm} \sin \omega t = 36 + 8 \sin \omega t \text{ mA}$$

where I_{dm} is the amplitude of the sinusoidal term.

Diode Applications

Rectifier circuits are two-port networks that capitalize on the nearly one-way conduction of the diode. An ac voltage is impressed upon the input port, and a dc voltage appears at the output port.

The simplest rectifier circuit (Fig. 2-11) contains a single diode. It is commonly called a *half-wave rectifier* because the diode conducts over either the positive or the negative halves of the input-voltage waveform.

Example 2.4 In Fig. 2-11, $v_S = C_m \sin \omega t$ and the diode is ideal. Calculate the average value of v_L.

Solution: Only one cycle of v_S need be considered. For the positive half-cycle, $i_D > 0$ and, by voltage division,

$$v_L = \frac{R_L}{R_L + R_S} (V_m \sin \omega t) \equiv V_{Lm} \sin \omega t$$

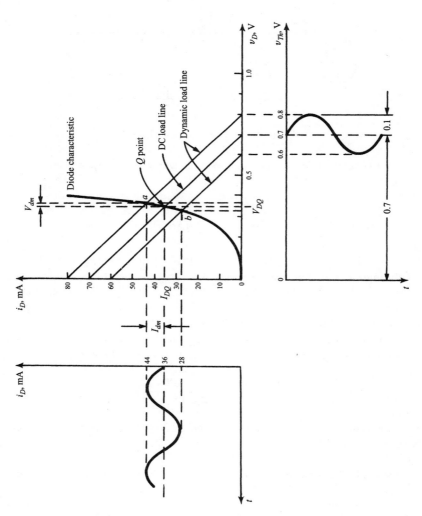

Fig. **2-10** dc/ac diode load-line example

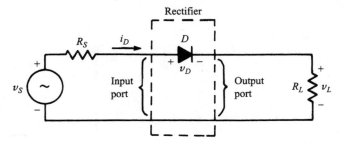

Fig. 2-11 Half-wave rectifier

For the negative half-cycle, the diode is reverse-biased, $i_D = 0$, and $v_L = 0$. Hence,

$$V_{L0} = \frac{1}{2\pi} \int_0^{2\pi} v_L(\omega t)\, d(\omega t) = \frac{1}{2\pi} \int_0^{\pi} V_{Lm} \sin \omega t\, d(\omega t) = \frac{V_{Lm}}{\pi}$$

Although, the half-wave rectifier gives a dc output, current flows through R_L only half the time, and the average value of the output voltage is only $1/\pi = 0.318$ times the peak value of the sinusoidal input voltage. The output voltage can be improved by use of a *full-wave rectifier*.

When rectifiers are used as dc power supplies, it is desirable that the average value of the output voltage remains nearly constant as the load varies. The degree of constancy is measured as the *voltage regulation*,

$$\text{Reg} \equiv \frac{(\text{no-load } V_{L0}) - (\text{full-load } V_{L0})}{\text{full-load } V_{L0}}$$

which is usually expressed as a percentage. Note that 0 percent implies a constant output voltage.

Example 2.5 Find the voltage regulation of the half-wave rectifier of Fig. 2-11.

Solution: From Example 2.4, we know that

$$\text{Full-load } V_{L0} = \frac{V_{Lm}}{\pi} = \frac{R_L}{\pi(R_L + R_S)} V_m$$

Realizing that $R_L \to \infty$ for no load, we may write

$$\text{No-load } V_{L0} = \lim_{R_L \to \infty} \left| \frac{R_L}{\pi(R_L + R_S)} V_m \right| = \frac{V_m}{\pi}$$

Thus, the voltage regulation is

$$\text{Reg} = \frac{\dfrac{V_m}{\pi} - \dfrac{R_L}{\pi(R_L + R_S)} V_m}{\dfrac{R_L}{\pi(R_L + R_S)} V_m} = \frac{R_S}{R_L} = \frac{100 R_S}{R_L} \%$$

The output of a rectifier alone does not usually suffice as a power supply, due to its variation in time. The situation is improved by placing a *filter* between the rectifier and the load. The filter acts to suppress the harmonics from the rectified waveform and to preserve the dc component. A measure of goodness for rectified waveforms is the *ripple factor,*

$$F_r \equiv \frac{\text{maximum variation in output voltage}}{\text{average value of output voltage}} = \frac{\Delta v_L}{V_{L0}}$$

A small value, say $F_r \le 0.05$ is usually attainable and practical.

Example 2.6 Calculate the ripple factor for the half-wave rectifier with filtering capacitor (see Fig. 2-12).

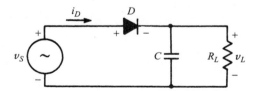

Fig. 2-12 Half-wave rectifier with shunt capacitor

Solution: The capacitor in Fig. 2-12 stores energy, while the diode allows current to flow, and delivers energy to the load when current flow is blocked. The actual load voltage v_L that results with the filter is sketched in Fig. 2-13, for which we assume that $v_S = V_{Sm} \sin \omega t$ and D is an ideal diode. For $0 < t \le t_1$, D is forward biased and capacitor C charges to the value V_{Sm}. For $t_1 < t \le t_2$, v_S is less than v_L, reverse-biasing D and caus-

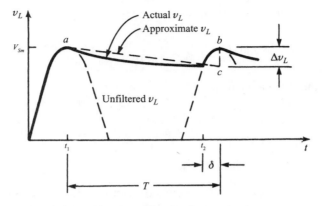

Fig. 2-13 Filtered output of a half-wave rectifier

ing it to act as an open circuit. During this interval, the capacitor is discharging through the load R_L, giving

$$v_L = V_{Sm}e^{-(t-t_1)/R_LC}, t_1 < t \leq t_2 \qquad (2.3)$$

Over the interval $t_2 < t \leq t_2 + \delta$, v_S forward-biases diode D and again charges the capacitor to V_{Sm}. Then v_S falls below the value of v_L and another discharge cycle identical to the first occurs.

Obviously, if the time constant R_LC is large enough compared to T to result in a decay like that indicated in Fig. 2-13, a major reduction in Δv_L and a major increase in V_{L0} will have been achieved, relative to an unfiltered rectifier. The introduction of two quite reasonable approximations leads to simple formulas for Δv_L and V_{L0} and, hence for F_r, that are sufficiently accurate for design and analysis work:

1. If Δv_L is to be small, then $\delta \to 0$ in Fig. 2-13 and $t_2 - t_1 \approx T$
2. If Δv_L is small enough, then (2.3) can be represented over the interval $t_1 < t \leq t_2$ by a straight line with a slope of magnitude V_{Sm}/R_LC.

The dashed line labeled "Approximate v_L" in Fig. 2-13 implements these two approximations. From right triangle abc,

$$\frac{\Delta v_L}{T} = \frac{V_{Sm}}{R_LC} \qquad \text{or} \qquad \Delta v_L = \frac{V_{Sm}}{fR_LC}$$

where f is the frequency of v_S. Since, under this approximation,

$$V_{L0} = V_{Sm} - \tfrac{1}{2}\Delta v_L$$

and $R_L C/T = f R_L C$ is presumed large,

$$F_r = \frac{\Delta v_L}{V_{L0}} = \frac{2}{2 f R_L C - 1} \approx \frac{1}{f R_L C}$$

Zener Diodes

The *Zener diode* or *reference diode*, whose symbol is shown in Fig. 2-14(*a*), finds primary usage as a voltage regulator or reference. The forward conduction characteristic of a Zener diode is much the same as that of a rectifier diode. However, it usually operates with a reverse bias, for which its characteristic is radically different.

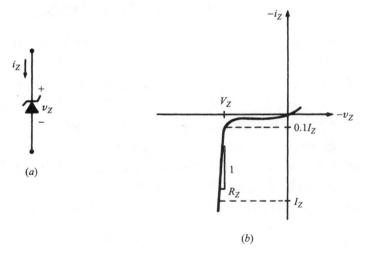

Fig. **2-14** Zener diode symbol and typical *vi*-curve

Note in Fig. 2-14(*b*) that:

1. The reverse breakdown is rather sharp. The breakdown voltage can be controlled through the manufacturing process so that it has a reasonably predictable value.

2. When a Zener diode is in reverse breakdown, its voltage remains extremely close to the breakdown value while the current varies from rated current (I_Z) to 10 percent or less of rated current.

A Zener regulator should be designed so that $i_Z \geq 0.1 I_Z$ to ensure the constancy of v_Z.

Example 2.7 Find the voltage v_Z across the Zener diode of Fig. 2-14(a) if $i_Z = 10$ mA and it is known that $V_Z = 5.6$ V, $I_Z = 25$ mA, and $R_Z = 10\Omega$.

Solution: Since $0.1 I_Z \leq i_Z \leq I_Z$, operation is along the safe and predictable region of Zener operation. Consequently,

$$v_Z \approx V_Z + i_Z R_Z = 5.6 + (10 \times 10^{-3})(10) = 5.7 \text{ V}$$

R_Z is frequently neglected in the design of Zener regulators.

Important Things to Remember

✔ Diodes conduct electric current when they are forward biased.

✔ Diodes block the flow when they are reverse biased.

✔ Load line analysis can be used to solve for a diode's voltage and current in a given circuit.

✔ One of the most common uses for diodes is in constructing rectifying circuits.

✔ Zener diodes are commonly used as voltage references.

Additional Solved Problems

ASP 2.1 A Ge diode described by (2.1) is operated at a junction temperature of 27°C. For a forward current of 10 mA, v_D is found to be 0.3 V. (a) If $v_D = 0.4$ V, find the forward current. (b) Find the reverse saturation current.

Solution: We form the ratio

$$\frac{i_{D2}}{i_{D1}} = \frac{I_0(e^{v_{D2}/V_T} - 1)}{I_0(e^{v_{D1}/V_T} - 1)} = \frac{I_0(e^{0.4/0.02587} - 1)}{I_0(e^{0.3/0.02587} - 1)} = 47.73$$

Then

$$i_{D2} = (47.73)(10 \text{ mA}) = 477.3 \text{ mA}$$

(*b*) By (2.1),

$$I_0 = \frac{i_{D1}}{I_0(e^{v_{D1}/V_T} - 1)} = \frac{10 \times 10^{-3}}{e^{0.3/0.02587} - 1} = 91 \text{ nA}$$

ASP 2.2 For the circuit of Fig. 2-15, sketch the waveforms of v_L and v_D if the source voltage v_S is as given in Fig. 2-16. The diode is ideal, and $R_L = 100 \ \Omega$.

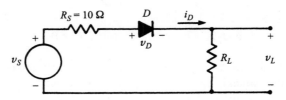

Fig. 2-15 Circuit for ASP 2.2

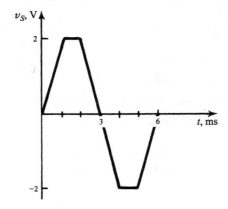

Fig. 2-16 Input waveform for ASP 2.2

Solution: If $v_S \geq 0$, D conducts so that $v_D = 0$ and

$$v_L = \frac{R_L}{R_L + R_S} v_S = \frac{100}{100 + 10} v_S = 0.909 v_S$$

If $v_S < 0$, D blocks so that $v_D = v_S$ and $v_D = 0$. Sketches of v_D and v_L are shown in Fig. 2-17.

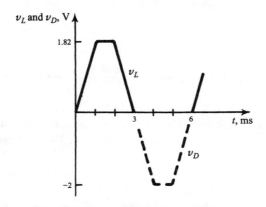

Fig. 2-17 Output waveforms for ASP 2.2

ASP 2.3 Sketch the i-v input characteristic of the network of Fig. 2-18 when (*a*) the switch is open and (*b*) the switch is closed.

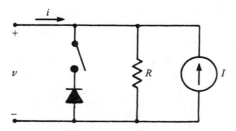

Fig. 2-18 Circuit for ASP 2.3

Solution: The solution is more easily found if the current source and resistor are replaced with the Thévenin equivalents $V_{Th} = IR$ and $R_{Th} = R$.

(a) KVL gives $v = iR_{Th} + IR$, which is the equation of a straight line intersecting the i-axis at $-I$ and the v-axis at IR. The slope of the line is $1/R$. The characteristic is sketched in Fig. 2-19(a).

(b) The diode is reverse-biased and acts as an open circuit when $v > 0$. It follows that the i-v characteristic here is identical to that with the switch open if $v \leq 0$. But if $v_S \leq 0$, the diode is forward-biased, acting as a short circuit. Consequently, v can never reach the negative values and the current i can increase negatively without limit. The corresponding i-v plot is sketched in Fig. 2-19(b).

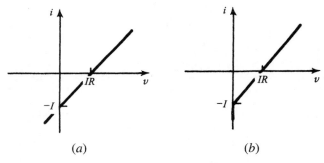

Fig. 2-19 (a) Open-switch v-i curve; (b) Closed-switch v-i curve

ASP 2.4 The Zener diode in the voltage-regulator of Fig. 2-20 has a constant reverse breakdown voltage $V_Z = 8.2$ V for 75 mA $\leq i_Z \leq 1$A. If $R_L = 9\ \Omega$, size R_S so that $v_L = V_Z$ is regulated to (maintained at) 8.2 V while V_b varies by ±10 percent from its nominal value of 12 V.

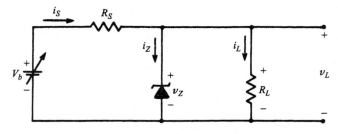

Fig. 2-20 Regulator circuit for ASP 2.4

Solution: By Ohm's law,

$$i_L = \frac{v_L}{R_L} = \frac{V_Z}{R_L} = \frac{8.2}{9} = 0.911 \text{ A}$$

Now an application of KVL gives

$$R_S = \frac{V_b - V_Z}{i_Z + i_L} \tag{A.1}$$

and we use (A.1) to size R_S for maximum Zener current I_Z at the largest value of V_b:

$$R_S = \frac{(1.1)(12) - 8.2}{1 + 0.911} = 2.62\,\Omega$$

Now we check to see if $i_z \geq 75$mA at the lowest value of V_b:

$$i_Z = \frac{V_b - v_Z}{R_S} - i_L = \frac{(0.9)(12) - 8.2}{2.62} - 0.911 = 81.3\text{mA}$$

Since $i_z \geq 75$mA, $v_Z = V_Z = 8.2$ V and regulation is preserved.

Chapter 3
CHARACTERISTICS OF BIPOLAR JUNCTION TRANSISTORS

IN THIS CHAPTER:

✔ *BJT Construction and Terminal Characteristics*

✔ *Current Relationships*

✔ *Bias and DC Load Lines*

✔ *Capacitors and AC Load Lines*

BJT Construction and Terminal Characteristics

The *bipolar junction transistor* (BJT) is a three-element (*emitter, base,* and *collector*) device made up of alternating layers of *n*- and *p*-type semiconductor materials joined metallurgically. The transistor can be of *pnp* type (principal conduction by positive holes) or of *npn* type (principal conduction by electrons), as shown in Fig. 3-1 (where schematic symbols and positive current directions are also shown). The double-subscript notation is utilized in labeling terminal voltages, so that, for example, v_{BE} symbolizes the increase in potential from emitter terminal E to base terminal B. For reasons that will be come apparent, terminal currents and

41

voltages commonly consist of superimposed dc and ac components (usually sinusoidal signals). Table 3-1 presents the notation for terminal voltages and currents.

Type of Value	Symbol		Examples
	Variable	Subscript	
total instantaneous	lowercase	uppercase	i_B, v_{BE}
dc	uppercase	uppercase	I_B, V_{BE}
quiescent-point	uppercase	uppercase plus Q	I_{BQ}, V_{BEQ}
ac instantaneous	lowercase	lowercase	i_b, v_{be}
rms	uppercase	lowercase	I_b, V_{be}
maximum (sinusoid)	uppercase	lowercase plus m	I_{bm}, V_{bem}

Table 3-1

Example 3.1 In the *npn* transistor of Fig. 3-1(*a*), 10^8 holes/μs move from the base to the emitter region, while 10^{10} electrons/ μs move from the emitter to the base region. An ammeter reads the base current as $i_B = 16$ μA. Determine the emitter current i_E and the collector current i_C.

Solution: The emitter current is found as the net flow of positive charge into the emitter region:

$$i_E = (1.602 \times 10^{-19} \text{ C/hole})(10^{14} \text{ holes/s}) - (-1.602 \times 10^{-19} \text{ C/electron})(10^{16} \text{ electrons/s})$$

$$= 1.602 \times 10^{-5} + 1.602 \times 10^{-3} = 1.618 \text{ mA}$$

Further, by KCL,

$$i_C = i_E - i_B = 1.618 \times 10^{-3} - 16 \times 10^{-6} = 1.602 \text{ mA}$$

The *common-base* (CB) connection is a two-port transistor arrangement in which the base shares a common point with the input and output terminals. The independent input variables are emitter current i_E and base-to-emitter voltage v_{EB}. The corresponding independent output variables are collector current i_C and base-to-collector voltage v_{CB}. Practical CB transistor analysis is based on two experimentally determined sets of curves:

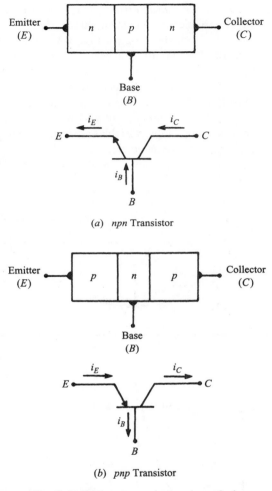

(a) *npn* Transistor

(b) *pnp* Transistor

Fig. 3-1 BJT construction and symbols

1. *Input* or *transfer characteristics* relate i_E and v_{EB} (port input variables), with v_{CB} (port output variable) held constant. The method of laboratory measurement is indicated in Fig. 3-2(a), and the typical form of the resulting family of curves is depicted in Fig. 3-2(b).

2. *Output* or *collector characteristics* give i_C as a function of v_{CB} (port output variables) for constant values of i_E (port input variable), measured as in Fig. 3-2(a). Fig. 3-2(c) shows the typical form of the resulting family of curves.

The *common-emitter* (*CE*) connection is a two-port transistor arrangement (widely used because of its high current amplification) in which the emitter shares a common point with the input and output terminals. The independent port input variables are base current i_B and emitter-to-base voltage v_{BE}, and the independent port output variables are collector current i_C and emitter-to-collector voltage v_{CE}. Like CB analysis, CE analysis is based on:

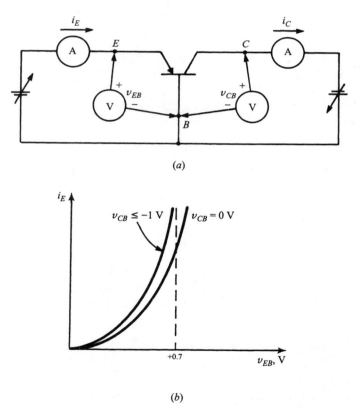

(a)

(b)

Fig. 3-2 Common-base characteristics (*pnp*, Si-device)

1. *Input* or *transfer characteristics* that relate the port input variables i_B and v_{BE}, with v_{CE} remaining constant. Fig. 3-3(a) shows the measurement setup, and Fig. 3-3(b) the resulting input characteristics.

2. *Output* or *collector characteristics* that show the functional relationship between port output variables i_C and v_{CE} for constant i_B, measured as in Fig. 3-3(a). Typical collector characteristics are displayed in Fig. 3-3(c).

Current Relationships

The two *pn* junctions of the BJT can be independently biased, to result in four possible transistor *operating modes* as summarized in Table 3-2. A junction is forward-biased if the *n* material is at a lower potential than the *p* material, and reverse-biased if the *n* material is at a higher potential than the *p* material.

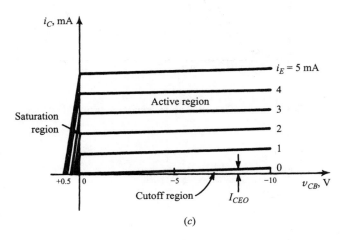

(c)

Fig. 3-2 Continued

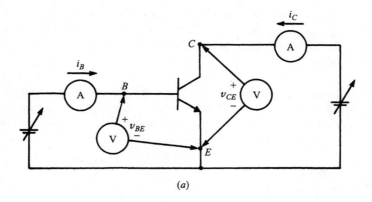

(a)

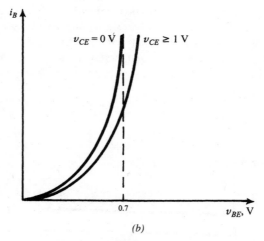

(b)

Fig. 3-3 Common-emitter characteristics (*npn*, Si device)

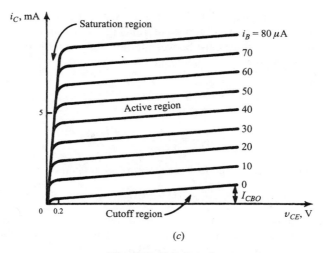

(c)

Fig. 3-3 Continued

Emitter-Base Bias	Collector-Base Bias	Operating Mode
forward	forward	saturation
reverse	reverse	cutoff
reverse	forward	inverse
forward	reverse	linear or active

Table 3-2

Saturation denotes operation (with $|v_{CE}| \approx 0.2$V and $|v_{BC}| \approx 0.5$V for Si devices) such that maximum collector current flows and the transistor acts much like a closed switch from collector to emitter terminals (see Figs. 3-2(c) and 3-3(c)).

Cutoff denotes operation near the voltage axis of the collector characteristics, where the transistor acts much like an open switch. Only leakage current (similar to I_o of the diode) flows in this mode of operation. Thus, $i_C = I_{CE0} \approx 0$ for a CB connection and $i_C = I_{CB0} \approx 0$ for a CE connection. Figures 3-2(c) and 3-3(c) indicate these leakage currents.

The *inverse* mode is a little-used, inefficient active mode with the emitter and collector interchanged.

The *active* or *linear* mode describes transistor operation in the region to the right of saturation and above cutoff in Figs. 3-2(c) and 3-3(c). Here, near-linear relationships exist between terminal currents. The following constants of proportionality are defined for dc currents:

$$\alpha(\equiv h_{FB}) \equiv \frac{I_C - I_{CB0}}{I_E} \tag{3.1}$$

$$\beta(\equiv h_{FE}) \equiv \frac{\alpha}{1-\alpha} \equiv \frac{I_C - I_{CE0}}{I_B} \tag{3.2}$$

where thermally generated leakage currents are related by

$$I_{CE0} = (\beta + 1)I_{CB0} \tag{3.3}$$

The constant $\alpha < 1$ is a measure of the proportion of majority carriers (holes for *pnp* devices, electrons for *npn* devices) injected into the base region from the emitter that are received by the collector.

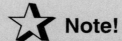

Note!

Equation (3.2) is the dc current amplification characteristic of the BJT.

Except for the leakage current, the base current is increased or amplified β times to become the collector current. Under dc conditions, KCL gives

$$I_E = I_C + I_B$$

which, in conjunction with (3.1) through (3.3), completely describes the dc current relationships in the active mode.

Example 3.2 Determine α and β for the transistor of Example 3.1 if the leakage currents (flow due to holes) are negligible and the described charge flow is constant.

Solution: If we assume $I_{CE0} = I_{CB0} = 0$, then

$$\alpha = \frac{i_C}{i_E} = \frac{i_E - i_B}{i_E} = \frac{1.602 - 0.016}{1.602} = 0.99$$

$$\beta = \frac{i_C}{i_B} = \frac{i_E - i_B}{i_B} = \frac{1.602 - 0.016}{0.016} = 99.125$$

Example 3.3 A BJT has $\alpha = 0.99$, $i_B = I_B = 25$ μA, and $I_{CB0} = 200$ nA. Find (a) the dc collector current, (b) the dc emitter current, and (c) the percentage error in the emitter current when leakage current is neglected.

Solution: (a) With $\alpha = 0.99$, (3.2) gives

$$\beta = \frac{\alpha}{1 - \alpha} = 99$$

Using (3.3) in (3.2) then gives

$$I_C = \beta I_B + (\beta + 1)I_{CB0} = 99(25 \times 10^{-6}) + (99 + 1)(200 \times 10^{-9}) = 2.495 \text{ mA}$$

(b) The dc emitter current follows from (3.1):

$$I_E = \frac{I_C - I_{CB0}}{\alpha} = \frac{2.495 \times 10^{-3} - 200 \times 10^{-9}}{0.99} = 2.518 \text{ mA}$$

(c) Neglecting the leakage current, we have

$$I_C = \beta I_B = 99(25 \times 10^{-6}) = 2.475 \text{ mA}$$

so

$$I_E = \frac{I_C}{\alpha} = \frac{2.475}{0.99} = 2.5 \text{ mA}$$

giving an emitter-current error of

$$\frac{2.518 - 2.5}{2.518}(100) = 0.71\%$$

Bias and DC Load Lines

Supply voltages and resistors *bias* a transistor. That is, they establish a specific set of dc terminal currents and voltages, thus, determining a point of active-mode operation (called the *quiescent point* or *Q point*). Usually, quiescent values are unchanged by the application of an ac signal to the circuit.

With the universal bias arrangement of Fig. 3-4(a), only one dc power supply (V_{CC}) is needed to establish active-mode operation. Use of the Thévenin equivalent of the circuit to the left of a,b leads to the circuit of Fig. 3-4(b), where

$$R_B = \frac{R_1 R_2}{R_1 + R_2} \qquad V_{BB} = \frac{R_1}{R_1 + R_2} V_{CC}$$

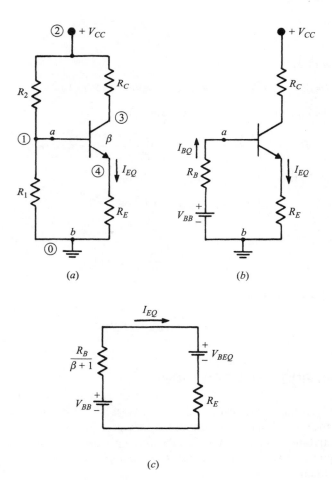

(a) (b)

(c)

Fig. 3-4 *npn* transistor biasing example

If we neglect leakage current so that $I_{EQ} = (\beta + 1)I_{BQ}$ and assume the emitter-to-base voltage V_{BEQ} is constant (≈ 0.7 V and 0.3 V for Si and Ge, respectively), then KVL around the emitter loop of Fig. 3-4(b) yields

$$V_{BB} = \frac{I_{EQ}}{\beta+1} R_B + V_{BEQ} + I_{EQ}R_E \qquad (3.4)$$

which can be represented by the emitter-loop equivalent bias current of Fig. 3-4(c). Solving (3.4) for I_{EQ} and noting that

$$I_{EQ} = \frac{I_{CQ}}{\alpha} \approx I_{CQ}$$

we obtain

$$I_{CQ} \approx I_{EQ} = \frac{V_{BB} - V_{BEQ}}{R_B / (\beta + 1) + R_E}$$

If component values and the worst-case β values are such that

$$\frac{R_B}{\beta + 1} \approx \frac{R_B}{\beta} << R_E$$

then I_{EQ} (and thus, I_{CQ}) is nearly constant, regardless of changes in β. The circuit then has β-independent bias.

From Fig. 3-3(c), it is apparent that the family of collector characteristics is described by the mathematical relationship $i_C = f(v_{CE}, i_B)$ with independent variable v_{CE} and the parameter i_B. We assume that the collector circuit can be biased so as to place the Q point anywhere in the active region. A typical setup is shown in Fig. 3-5 from which

$$I_{CQ} = -\frac{V_{CEQ}}{R_{dc}} + \frac{V_{CC}}{R_{dc}}$$

Thus, if the *dc load line*,

$$i_C = -\frac{v_{CE}}{R_{dc}} + \frac{V_{CC}}{R_{dc}} \qquad (3.5)$$

and the specification

$$i_B = I_{BQ}$$

are combined with the relationship for the collector characteristics, the resulting system can be solved (analytically or graphically) for the collector quiescent quantities I_{CQ} and V_{CEQ}.

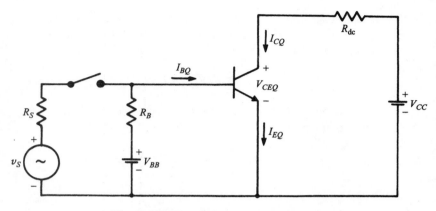

Fig. 3-5 BJT transistor circuit example

Example 3.4 The signal source switch of Fig. 3-5 is closed, and the transistor base current becomes

$$i_B = I_{BQ} + i_b = 40 + 20\sin\omega t \ \mu A$$

The collector characteristics of the transistor are those displayed in Fig. 3-6. If $V_{CC} = 12$ V and $R_{dc} = 1$ kΩ, graphically determine (a) I_{CQ} and V_{CEQ}, (b) i_c and v_{ce}, and (c) $h_{fe}(=\beta)$ at the Q point.

Solution: (a) The dc load has ordinate intercept $V_{CC}/R_{dc} = 12$ mA and abscissa intercept $V_{CC} = 12$ V and is constructed on Fig. 3-6. The Q point is the intersection of the load line with the characteristic curve $i_B = I_{BQ} = 40 \ \mu A$. The collector quiescent quantities may be read from the axes as $I_{CQ} = 4.9$ mA and $V_{CEQ} = 7.2$ V.

(b) A time scale is constructed perpendicular to the load line at the Q point, and a scaled sketch of $i_b = 20\sin\omega t \ \mu A$ is drawn (see Fig. 3-6) and translated through the load line to a sketch of i_c to the left of the BJT characteristic axes. As i_b swings $\pm 20 \ \mu A$ along the load line from points a to b, the ac components of collector current and voltage take on the values of ± 2.25 mA and ∓ 2.37 V. The time-varying expressions for the current and voltage are

$$i_c = 2.25\sin\omega t \text{ mA} \quad \text{and} \quad v_{cw} = -2.37 \sin\omega t \text{ V}$$

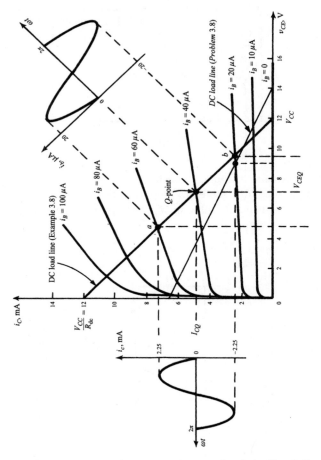

Fig. 3-6 Characteristic curves for the circuit in Fig. 3-5

The negative sign on v_{ce} indicates that it is 180 degrees out of phase with i_b and i_c.

(c) From (3.2) with $I_{CE0} = 0$ (the $i_B = 0$ curve coincides with the v_{CE} axis in Fig. 3-6),

$$h_{FE} = \frac{I_{CQ}}{I_{BQ}} = \frac{4.9 \times 10^{-3}}{40 \times 10^{-6}} = 122.5$$

Class	Percentage of Active-Region Signal Excursion
A	100
AB	between 50 and 100
B	50
C	less than 50

Table 3-3

It is clear that amplifiers can be biased for operation at any point along the dc load line. Table 3-3 shows the various classes of amplifiers, based on the percentage of the signal cycle over which they operate in the linear or active region.

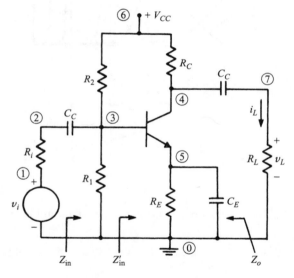

Fig. 3-7 BJT circuit with capacitors

Capacitors and AC Load Lines

Two common uses of capacitors (sized to appear as short circuits to signal frequencies) are illustrated by the circuit of Fig. 3-7.

1. Coupling capacitors (C_C) confine dc quantities to the transistor and its bias circuitry.
2. Bypass capacitors (C_E) effectively remove the gain-reducing emitter resistor R_E insofar as signals are concerned, while allowing R_E to play its role in establishing β-independent bias.

The capacitors of Fig. 3-7 are shorted in the circuit as it appears to ac signals (see Fig. 3-8). In Fig. 3-7, we note that the collector-circuit resistance seen by the dc bias current $\approx I_{EQ}$ and $R_{dc} = R_C + R_E$. However, from Fig. 3-8, it is apparent that the collector-signal current i_c sees a collector-circuit resistance $R_{ac} = R_C R_L / (R_C + R_L)$. Since $R_{ac} \neq R_{dc}$ in general, the concept of an *ac load line* arises. By application of KVL to Fig. 3-8, the v-i characteristic of the external signal circuitry is found to be

$$v_{ce} = i_c R_{ac} \tag{3.6}$$

Since $i_c = i_C - I_{CQ}$ and $v_{ce} = v_{CE} - V_{CEQ}$, (3.6) can be written analogously to (3.5) as

$$i_C = -\frac{v_{CE}}{R_{ac}} + \frac{V_{CEQ}}{R_{ac}} + I_{CQ} \tag{3.7}$$

All excursions of the ac signals i_c and v_{ce} are represented by points on the ac load line (3.7). If the value $i_C = I_{CQ}$ is substituted into (3.7), we find that $v_{CE} = V_{CEQ}$. Thus, the ac load line intersects the dc load line at the Q point.

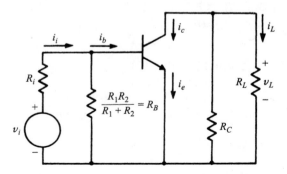

Fig. 3-8 CE amplifier with capacitors shorted

Example 3.5 Find the point at which the ac load line intersects the axes of the collector characteristic.

Solution: The i_C intercept ($i_{C\max}$) is found by setting $v_{CE} = 0$ in (3.7):

$$i_{C\max} = \frac{V_{CEQ}}{R_{ac}} + I_{CQ}$$

The v_{CE} intercept is found by setting $i_C = 0$ in (3.7):

$$v_{CE\max} = V_{CEQ} + I_{CQ}R_{ac}$$

Important Things to Remember

✔ Bipolar junction transistors are three-terminal semiconductor devices.

✔ The most common connections for the BJT are the common base (CB) and common emitter (CE).

✔ Near linear relationships exist between the terminal currents in the active region.

✔ The dc biasing determines the quiescent point of operation for the BJT.

✔ Capacitors can be used to confine the dc quantities to the BJT and bias circuitry.

Additional Solved Problems

ASP 3.1 The transistor of Fig. 3-9 has $\alpha = 0.98$ and a base current of 30 µA. Find (a) β, (b) I_{CQ}, and (c) I_{EQ}. Assume negligible leakage current.

Solution: (a) $\quad \beta = \dfrac{\alpha}{1-\alpha} = \dfrac{0.98}{1-0.98} = 49$

(b) From (3.2) with $I_{CE0} = 0$, we have

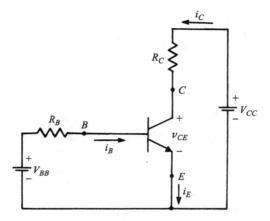

Fig. 3-9 Circuit for ASP 3.1

$$I_{CQ} = \beta I_{BQ} = (49)(30 \times 10^{-6}) = 1.47 \text{ mA}$$

(*c*) From (3.1) with $I_{CB0} = 0$,

$$I_{EQ} = \frac{I_{CQ}}{\alpha} = \frac{1.47}{0.98} = 1.50 \text{ mA}$$

ASP 3.2 The transistor of Fig. 3-10 is a Si device with a base current of 40 μA and $I_{CB0} = 0$. If $V_{BB} = 6V$, $R_E = 1k\Omega$, and $\beta = 80$, find (*a*) I_{EQ} and (*b*) R_B. (*c*) If $V_{CC} = 15V$ and $R_C = 3k\Omega$, find V_{CEQ}.

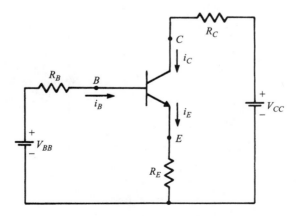

Fig. 3-10 Circuit for ASP 3.2

Solution: (a) $\alpha = \dfrac{\beta}{\beta+1} = \dfrac{80}{81} = 0.9876$

Then, combining (3.1) and (3.2) with $I_{CB0} = I_{CE0} = 0$ gives

$$I_{EQ} = \frac{I_{BQ}}{1-\alpha} = \frac{40 \times 10^{-6}}{1-0.9876} = 3.226 \text{ mA}$$

(b) Applying KVL around the base-emitter loop gives

$$V_{BB} = I_{BQ}R_B + V_{BEQ} + I_{EQ}R_E$$

Or (with V_{BEQ} equal to the usual 0.7 V for a Si device)

$$R_B = \frac{V_{BB} - V_{BEQ} - I_{EQ}R_E}{I_{BQ}} = \frac{6-0.7-(3.226)(1)}{40 \times 10^{-6}} = 51.85 \text{ k}\Omega$$

(c) From (3.2) with $I_{CE0} = 0$,

$$I_{CQ} = \beta I_{BQ} = (80)(40 \times 10^{-6}) = 3.2 \text{ mA}$$

Then, by KVL,

$$V_{CEQ} = V_{CC} - I_{EQ}R_E - I_{CQ}R_C = 15 - (3.226)(1) - (3.2)(3) = 2.174 \text{ V}$$

ASP 3.3 The Si transistor of Fig. 3-11 is biased for constant base current. If $\beta = 80$, $V_{CEQ} = 8$V, $R_C = 3$kΩ, and $V_{CC} = 15$V, find (a) I_{CQ} and (b) the required value of R_B. (c) Find R_B if the transistor is a Ge device.

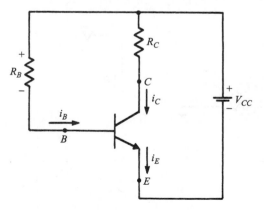

Fig. 3-11 Circuit for ASP 3.3

Solution: (a) By KVL around the collector-emitter circuit,

$$I_{CQ} = \frac{V_{CC} - V_{CEQ}}{R_C} = \frac{15 - 8}{3 \times 10^3} = 2.333 \text{ mA}$$

(b) If leakage current is neglected, (3.2) gives

$$I_{BQ} = \frac{I_{CQ}}{\beta} = \frac{2.333 \times 10^{-3}}{80} = 29.16 \ \mu\text{A}$$

Since the transistor is a Si device, $V_{BEQ} = 0.7$ V and, by KVL around the outer loop,

$$R_B = \frac{V_{CC} - V_{BEQ}}{I_{BQ}} = \frac{15 - 0.7}{29.16 \times 10^{-6}} = 490.4 \text{ k}\Omega$$

(c) The only difference here is that $V_{BEQ} = 0.3$ V. Thus,

$$R_B = \frac{15 - 0.3}{29.16 \times 10^{-6}} = 504.1 \text{ k}\Omega$$

Chapter 4
SMALL-SIGNAL MIDFREQUENCY BJT AMPLIFIERS

IN THIS CHAPTER:

✔ *Introduction*
✔ *Hybrid-Parameter Models*
✔ *Measures of Amplifier Goodness*
✔ *CE Amplifier Analysis*
✔ *CB Amplifier Analysis*
✔ *CC Amplifier Analysis*

Introduction

For sufficiently small emitter-collector voltage and current excursions about the quiescent point (*small signals*), the BJT is considered linear. It may then be replaced with any of several two-port networks of impedances and controlled sources (called *small-signal equivalent-circuit models*), to which standard network analysis methods are applicable. Moreover, there is a range of signal frequencies that are large enough so that coupling or bypass capacitors can be considered short circuits, yet low enough so that inherent capacitive reactances associated with BJTs can be considered open circuits. In this chapter, all BJT voltage and current signals are assumed to be in this *midfrequency range.*

Note!

In general, the design of small-signal amplifiers is divided into two parts: (1) setting the dc bias or Q point, and (2) determining voltage- or current-gain ratios and impedance values at signal frequencies.

Hybrid-Parameter Models

General hybrid-parameter analysis of two-port networks was introduced in Chapter 1. Actually, different sets of h parameters are defined, depending on which element of the transistor (E, B, or C) shares a common point with the amplifier input and output terminals.

Common-Emitter Transistor Connection
From Fig. 3-3(b) and (c), we see that if i_C and v_{BE} are taken as dependent variables in the CE transistor configuration, then

$$v_{BE} = f_1(i_B, v_{CE}) \tag{4.1}$$

$$i_C = f_2(i_B, v_{CE}) \tag{4.2}$$

If the total emitter-to-base voltage v_{BE} goes through only *small* excursions (ac signals) about the Q point, then

$$v_{be} = \Delta v_{BE} \approx dv_{BE} = \left.\frac{\partial v_{BE}}{\partial i_B}\right|_Q i_b + \left.\frac{\partial v_{BE}}{\partial v_{CE}}\right|_Q v_{ce} \tag{4.3}$$

$$i_c = \Delta i_C \approx di_C = \left.\frac{\partial i_C}{\partial i_B}\right|_Q i_b + \left.\frac{\partial i_C}{\partial v_{CE}}\right|_Q v_{ce} \tag{4.4}$$

The four partial derivatives, evaluated at the Q point, that occur in (4.3) and (4.4), are called *CE hybrid parameters* and are denoted as follows:

Input resistance
$$h_{ie} \equiv \left.\frac{\partial v_{BE}}{\partial i_B}\right|_Q \approx \left.\frac{\Delta v_{BE}}{\Delta i_B}\right|_Q$$

Reverse voltage ratio
$$h_{re} \equiv \left. \frac{\partial v_{BE}}{\partial v_{CE}} \right|_Q \approx \left. \frac{\Delta v_{BE}}{\Delta v_{CE}} \right|_Q$$

Forward current gain
$$h_{fe} \equiv \left. \frac{\partial i_C}{\partial i_B} \right|_Q \approx \left. \frac{\Delta i_C}{\Delta i_B} \right|_Q$$

Output admittance
$$h_{oe} \equiv \left. \frac{\partial i_C}{\partial v_{CE}} \right|_Q \approx \left. \frac{\Delta i_C}{\Delta v_{CE}} \right|_Q$$

The equivalent circuit for (4.3) and (4.4) is shown in Fig. 4-1(a). The circuit is valid for use with signals whose excursions about the Q point are sufficiently small so that the h parameters may be treated as constants.

Common-Base Transistor Connection

If v_{EB} and i_C are taken as the dependent variables for the CB transistor characteristics of Fig. 3-2(b) and (c), then, as in the CE case, equations can be found specifically for small excursions about the Q point. The results are

$$v_{eb} = h_{ib}i_e + h_{rb}v_{cb} \tag{4.5}$$

$$i_c = h_{fb}i_e + h_{ob}v_{cb} \tag{4.6}$$

The partial-derivative definitions of the CB h-parameters are:

Input resistance
$$h_{ib} \equiv \left. \frac{\partial v_{EB}}{\partial i_E} \right|_Q \approx \left. \frac{\Delta v_{EB}}{\Delta i_E} \right|_Q$$

Reverse voltage ratio
$$h_{rb} \equiv \left. \frac{\partial v_{EB}}{\partial v_{CB}} \right|_Q \approx \left. \frac{\Delta v_{EB}}{\Delta v_{CB}} \right|_Q$$

Forward current gain
$$h_{fb} \equiv \left. \frac{\partial i_C}{\partial i_E} \right|_Q \approx \left. \frac{\Delta i_C}{\Delta i_E} \right|_Q$$

Output admittance
$$h_{ob} \equiv \left. \frac{\partial i_C}{\partial v_{CB}} \right|_Q \approx \left. \frac{\Delta i_C}{\Delta v_{CB}} \right|_Q$$

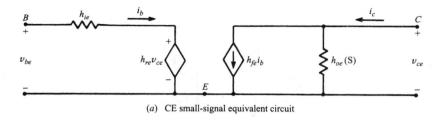

(*a*) CE small-signal equivalent circuit

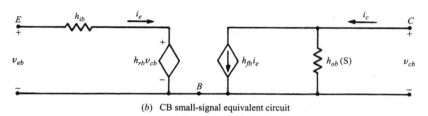

(*b*) CB small-signal equivalent circuit

Fig. 4-1 Hybrid parameter models for small signals

A small-signal, *h*-parameter equivalent circuit satisfying (4.5) and (4.6) is shown in Fig. 4-1(*b*).

Common-Collector Amplifier

The *common-collector* (CC) or *emitter-follower* (EF) amplifier, with the universal bias circuitry of Fig. 4-2(*a*), can be modeled for small-signal ac analysis by replacing the CE connected transistor with its *h*-parameter model of Fig. 4-1(*a*). Assuming, for simplicity, that $h_{re} = h_{oe} = 0$, we obtain the equivalent circuit of Fig. 4-2(*b*).

An even simpler model can be obtained by finding a Thévenin equivalent for the circuit to the right of *a,a* in Fig. 4-2(*b*). Application of KVL around the outer loop gives

$$v = i_b h_{ie} + i_e R_E + i_b h_{ie} + (h_{fe} + 1)i_b R_E$$

The Thévenin impedance is the driving-point impedance:

$$R_{Th} = \frac{v}{i_B} = h_{ie} + (h_{fe} + 1)R_E$$

The Thévenin voltage is zero (computed with terminals *a,a* open). Thus, the equivalent circuit consists only of R_{Th}. This is shown, in a base-current frame of reference, in Fig. 4-2(*c*).

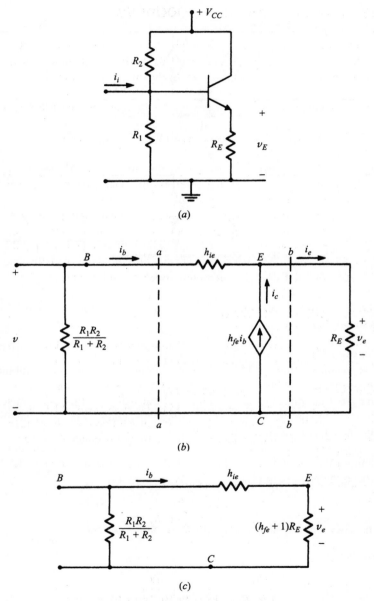

Fig. 4-2 CC amplifier

Measures of Amplifier Goodness

Amplifiers are usually designed to emphasize one or more of the following interrelated performance characteristics, whose quantitative measures of goodness are defined in terms of the quantities of Fig. 4-3.

1. *Current amplification*, measured by the current-gain ratio $A_i = i_o/i_{in}$.
2. *Voltage amplification*, measured by the voltage-gain ratio $A_v = v_o/v_{in}$.
3. *Power amplification*, measured by the ratio $A_p = A_v A_i = v_o i_o / v_{in} i_{in}$
4. *Phase shift of signals*, measured by the phase angle of the frequency-domain ratio $A_v(j\omega)$ or $A_i(j\omega)$
5. *Impedance match or change*, measured by the input impedance Z_{in} (the driving-point impedance looking into the input port).
6. *Power transfer ability*, measured by the output impedance Z_o (the driving-point impedance looking into the output port with the load removed). If $Z_o = Z_L$, maximum power transfer occurs.

CE Amplifier Analysis

A simplified (bias network omitted) CE amplifier is shown in Fig. 4.4(*a*) and the associated small-signal equivalent circuit in Fig. 4-4(*b*).

Example 4.1 In the CE amplifier of Fig. 4-4(*b*), let $h_{ie} = 1\text{k}\Omega$, $h_{re} = 10^{-4}$, $h_{fe} = 100$, $h_{oe} = 12\mu S$, and $R_L = 2\text{k}\Omega$. (These are typical CE amplifier values) Find expressions for the (*a*) current-gain ratio A_i, (*b*) voltage-gain ratio A_v, (*c*) input impedance Z_{in}, (*d*) output impedance Z_o, (*e*) evaluate this typical CE amplifier.

Solution: (*a*) By current division at node C,

$$i_L = \frac{1/h_{oe}}{1/h_{oe} + R_L}(-h_{fe}i_b)$$

and

$$A_i = \frac{i_L}{i_b} = \frac{-h_{fe}}{1 + h_{oe}R_L} = \frac{-100}{1 + (12 \times 10^{-6})(2 \times 10^3)} = -97.7$$

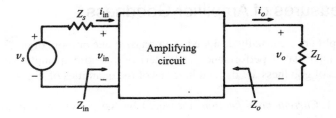

Fig. 4-3 Defining goodness measure quantities for amplifiers

Note that $A_i \approx -h_{fe}$, where the minus sign indicates a 180 degree phase shift between the input and output currents.

(b) By KVL around the B,E mesh,

$$v_s = v_{be} = h_{ie}i_b + h_{re}v_{ce} \qquad (4.7)$$

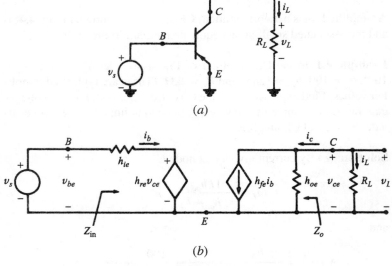

Fig. 4-4 Simplified small-signal CE amplifier

Ohm's law applied to the output network requires that

$$v_{ce} = -h_{fe}i_b\left(\frac{1}{h_{oe}} \parallel R_L\right) = \frac{-h_{fe}R_L i_b}{1 + h_{oe}R_L} \tag{4.8}$$

Solving (4.8) for i_b and substituting the result into (4.7), and rearranging yields

$$\begin{aligned}
A_v &= \frac{v_{ce}}{v_s} = \frac{-h_{fe}R_L}{h_{ie} + R_L(h_{ie}h_{oe} - h_{fe}h_{re})} \\
&= \frac{-(100)(2\times 10^3)}{1\times 10^3 + (2\times 10^3)[(1\times 10^3)(12\times 10^{-6}) - (100)(1\times 10^{-4})]} = -199.2
\end{aligned}$$

Observe that $A_v \approx -h_{fe}R_L/h_{ie}$, where the minus sign indicates a 180 degree phase shift between input and output voltages.

(c) Substituting (4.8) into (4.7) and rearranging yields

$$Z_{in} = \frac{v_s}{i_b} = h_{ie} - \frac{h_{re}h_{fe}R_L}{1 + h_{oe}R_L} = 1\times 10^3 - \frac{(1\times 10^{-4})(100)(2\times 10^3)}{1 + (12\times 10^{-6})(2\times 10^3)} = 980.5\,\Omega$$

Note that for typical CE amplifier values, $Z_{in} \approx h_{ie}$.

(d) We deactivate (short) v_s and replace R_L with a driving-point source so that $v_{dp} = v_{ce}$. Then, for the input mesh, Ohm's law requires that

$$i_b = -\frac{h_{re}}{h_{ie}}v_{dp} \tag{4.9}$$

However, at node C (with, now, $i_c = i_{dp}$), KCL yields

$$i_c = i_{dp} = h_{fe}i_b + h_{oe}v_{dp} \tag{4.10}$$

Using (4.9) in (4.10) and rearranging yields

$$Z_o = \frac{v_{dp}}{i_{dp}} = \frac{1}{h_{oe} - h_{fe}h_{re}/h_{ie}} = \frac{1}{(12\times 10^{-6}) - (100)(1\times 10^{-4})/(1\times 10^3)} = 500\,\mathrm{k\Omega}$$

The output impedance is increased by feedback due to the presence of the controlled source $h_{re}v_{ce}$.

(*e*) Based on the typical values of this example, the characteristics of the CE amplifier can be summarized as follows:

1. Large current gain
2. Large voltage gain
3. Large power gain $(A_i A_v)$
4. Current and voltage phase shifts of 180 degrees
5. Moderate input impedance
6. High output impedance

CB Amplifier Analysis

A simplified (bias network omitted) CB amplifier is shown in Fig. 4-5(*a*) and the associated small-signal equivalent circuit is shown in Fig. 4-5(*b*).

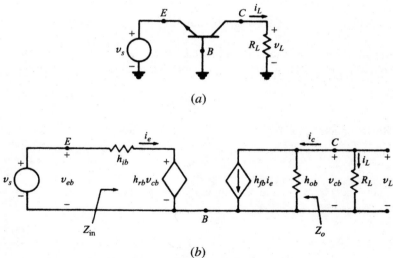

(*a*)

(*b*)

Fig. 4-5 Common base amplifier

Example 4.2 In the CB amplifier of Fig. 4-5(b), let $h_{ib} = 30\Omega$, $h_{rb} = 4 \times 10^{-6}$, $h_{fb} = -0.99$, $h_{ob} = 8 \times 10^{-7}$ S, and $R_L = 20$ kΩ. (These are typical CB amplifier values.) Find expressions for the (a) current-gain ratio A_i, (b) voltage-gain ratio A_v, (c) input impedance Z_{in}, (d) output impedance Z_o, (e) evaluate this typical CB amplifier.

Solution: (a) By direct analogy with Ex. 4.1(a),

$$A_i = \frac{-h_{fb}}{1 + h_{ob}R_L} = \frac{-(-0.99)}{1 + (8 \times 10^{-7})(20 \times 10^{3})} = 0.974$$

Note that $A_i \approx -h_{fb} < 1$ and that the input and output currents are in phase because $h_{fb} < 0$.

(b) By direct analogy with Ex. 4.1(b),

$$A_v = \frac{-h_{fb}R_L}{h_{ib} + R_L(h_{ib}h_{ob} - h_{fb}h_{rb})}$$

$$= \frac{-(-0.99)(20 \times 10^{3})}{30 + (20 \times 10^{3})[(30)(8 \times 10^{-7}) - (-0.99)(4 \times 10^{-6})]} = 647.9$$

Observe that $A \approx -h_{fb}R_L/h_{ib}$ and the output and input voltages are in phase because $h_{fb} < 0$.

(c) By direct analogy with Ex. 4.1(c),

$$Z_{in} = h_{ib} - \frac{h_{rb}h_{fb}R_L}{1 + h_{ob}R_L} = 30 - \frac{(4 \times 10^{-6})(-0.99)(20 \times 10^{3})}{1 + (8 \times 10^{-7})(20 \times 10^{3})} = 30.08\,\Omega$$

It is apparent that $Z_{in} \approx h_{ib}$.

(d) By direct analogy with Ex. 4.1(d),

$$Z_o = \frac{1}{h_{ob} - h_{fb}h_{rb}/h_{ib}} = \frac{1}{(8 \times 10^{-7}) - (-0.99)(4 \times 10^{-6})/(30)} = 1.07\,\text{M}\Omega$$

Note that Z_o is decreased because of the feedback from the output mesh to the input mesh through $h_{rb}v_{cb}$.

(*e*) Based on the typical values of this example, the characteristics of the CB amplifier can be summarized as follows:

1. Current gain less than unity
2. High voltage gain
3. Power gain approximately equal to the voltage gain
4. No phase shift for current or voltage
5. Small input impedance
6. Large output impedance

CC Amplifier Analysis

A simplified (bias network omitted) CC amplifier is shown in Fig. 4-6(*a*) and the associated small-signal equivalent circuit is shown in Fig. 4-6(*b*).

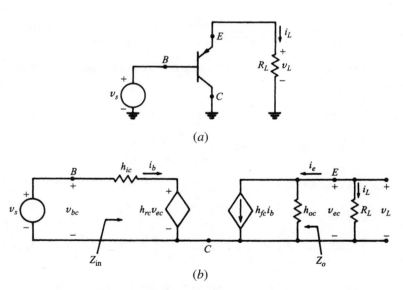

Fig. 4-6 Common collector amplifier

Example 4.3 In the CC amplifier of Fig. 4-6(b), let $h_{ic} = 1k\Omega$, $h_{rc} = 1$, $h_{fc} = -101$, $h_{ob} = 12 \mu S$ and $R_L = 2$ kΩ. (These are typical CC amplifier values) Drawing direct analogies with the CE amplifier of Example 4.1, find expressions for the (a) current-gain ratio A_i, (b) voltage-gain ratio A_v, (c) input impedance Z_{in}, (d) output impedance Z_o, (e) evaluate this typical CC amplifier.

Solution: (a) In parallel with Ex. 4.1(a),

$$A_i = -\frac{h_{fc}}{1+h_{oc}R_L} = -\frac{-101}{1+(12\times 10^{-6})(2\times 10^3)} = 98.6$$

Note that $A \approx -h_{fc}$ and that the input and output currents are in phase because $h_{fc} < 0$.

(b) In parallel with Ex. 4.1(b),

$$A_v = \frac{-h_{fc}R_L}{h_{ic} + R_L(h_{ic}h_{oc} - h_{fc}h_{rc})}$$

$$= \frac{-(-101)(2\times 10^3)}{1\times 10^3 + (2\times 10^3)[(1\times 10^3)(12\times 10^{-6}) - (-101)(1)]} = 0.995$$

Observe that $A_v \approx 1/(1 - h_{ic}h_{oc}/h_{fc}) \approx 1$. Since the gain is approximately 1 and the output voltage is in phase with the input voltage, this amplifier is commonly called a *unity follower*.

(c) In parallel with Ex. 4.1(c),

$$Z_{in} = h_{ic} - \frac{h_{rc}h_{fc}R_L}{1+h_{oc}R_L} = 1\times 10^3 - \frac{(1)(-101)(2\times 10^3)}{1+(12\times 10^{-6})(2\times 10^3)} = 198.3\,k\Omega$$

(d) In parallel with Ex. 4.1(d),

$$Z_o = \frac{1}{h_{oc} - h_{fc}h_{rc}/h_{ic}} = \frac{1}{(12\times 10^{-6}) - (-101)(1)/(1\times 10^3)} = 9.9\,\Omega$$

Note that $Z_o \approx -h_{ic}/h_{fc}$.

(*e*) Based on the typical values of this example, the characteristics of the CC amplifier can be summarized as follows:

1. High current gain
2. Voltage gain of approximately unity
3. Power gain approximately equal to the current gain
4. No phase shift for current or voltage
5. Large input impedance
6. Small output impedance

Important Things to Remember

✔ For sufficiently small signals, the response of the BJT is nearly linear, facilitating the use of network analysis.

✔ Hybrid parameters are used to define the two-port networks in CE, CB, and CC connections.

✔ Current, voltage, and power gains along with input and output impedances are some of the more important measures of amplifier goodness.

✔ CE amplifiers have good overall goodness measures.

✔ CB amplifiers generally have the highest voltage gain.

✔ CC amplifiers generally have the highest current gain.

Additional Solved Problems

ASP 4.1 Use a small-signal *h*-parameter equivalent circuit to analyze the amplifier of Fig. 3-7, given $R_C = R_L = 800\Omega$, $R_i = 0$, $R_1 = 1.2\text{k}\Omega$, $R_2 =$

$2.7k\Omega$, $h_{re} \approx 0$, $h_{oe} = 100\mu S$, $h_{fe} = 90$, and $h_{ie} = 200\Omega$. Calculate (*a*) the voltage gain A_v and (*b*) the current gain A_i.

Solution: (*a*) The small signal equivalent circuit is shown in Fig. 4-7, where

$$R_B = \frac{R_1 R_2}{R_1 + R_2} = 831 \ \Omega$$

By current division in the collector circuit,

$$-i_L = \frac{R_C(1/h_{oe})}{R_C(1/h_{oe}) + R_L(1/h_{oe}) + R_L R_C} h_{fe} i_b$$

The voltage gain is then

$$A_v \equiv \frac{v_L}{v_i} = \frac{R_L i_L}{h_{ie} i_b} = -\frac{h_{fe} R_L R_C}{h_{ie}(R_L + R_C + h_{oe} R_L R_C)}$$

$$= \frac{(90)(800)^2}{200[1600 + (100 \times 10^{-6})(800)^2]} = -173.08$$

(*b*) By current division,

$$i_b = \frac{R_B}{R_B + h_{ie}} i_i$$

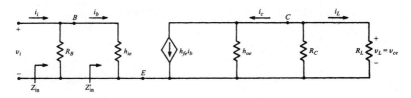

Fig. 4-7 Small-signal circuit for ASP 4.1.

So,

$$A_i \equiv \frac{i_L}{i_i} = \frac{R_B}{R_B + h_{ie}} \frac{i_L}{i_b} = \frac{R_B h_{ie}}{R_L(R_B + h_{ie})} A_v$$

$$= \frac{(831)(200)(-173.08)}{(800)(1031)} = -34.87$$

ASP 4.2 In the CB amplifier of Fig. 4-8(a), let $R_1 = R_2 = 50$ kΩ, $R_c = 2.2$ kΩ, $R_E = 3.3$ kΩ, $R_E = 1.1$ kΩ, $C_C = C_B \to \infty$, $h_{rb} \approx 0$, $h_{ib} = 25$Ω, $h_{oe} = 10^{-6}$ S, and $h_{fb} = -0.99$. Find and evaluate the expression for the voltage-gain ratio A_v.

Solution: With $h_{rb} = 0$, the CB h-parameter model of Fig. 4-1(b) can be used to draw the small-signal circuit of Fig. 4-8(b). By Ohm's law at the input mesh,

$$i_e = \frac{v_S}{h_{ib}} \tag{A.1}$$

Ohm's law at the output mesh requires

$$v_L = \left(\frac{1}{h_{ob}} \| R_C \| R_L \right)(-h_{fb}i_e) = -\frac{R_C R_L h_{fb} i_e}{R_C + R_L + h_{ob}R_C R_L} \tag{A.2}$$

Substitution of (A.1) into (A.2) allows the formation of A_v:

$$A_V = \frac{v_L}{v_S} = -\frac{R_C R_L h_{fb}}{h_{ib}(R_C + R_L + h_{ob}R_C R_L)}$$

$$= -\frac{(2.2 \times 10^3)(1.1 \times 10^3)(-0.99)}{25[2.2 \times 10^3 + 1.1 \times 10^3 + (10^{-6})(2.2 \times 10^3)(1.1 \times 10^3)]} = 29.02$$

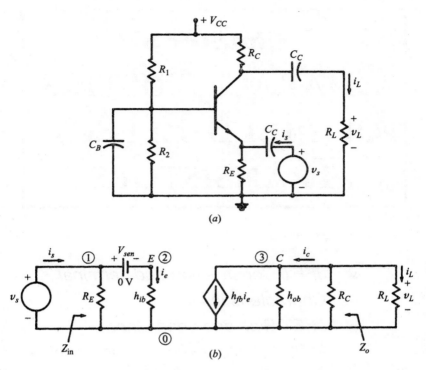

Fig. 4-8 (*a*) CB amplifier for ASP 4.2; (*b*) Small signal model

Chapter 5

CHARACTERISTICS OF FIELD-EFFECT TRANSISTORS

The operation of the *field-effect transistor* (FET) can be explained in terms of only majority-carrier (one-polarity) charge flow. The transistor is therefore called *unipolar*. Two kinds of field-effect devices are widely used: the *junction field-effect transistor* (JFET) and the *metal-oxide semiconductor-field-effect transistor* (MOSFET).

JFET Construction and Terminal Characteristics

The physical arrangement of, and symbols for, the two-kinds of JFET are shown in Fig. 5-1.

76

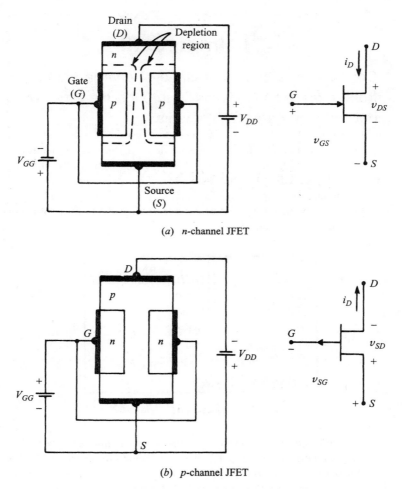

(a) n-channel JFET

(b) p-channel JFET

Fig. 5-1 Construction of JFET transistors

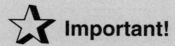

⭐ Important!

Conduction is by the passage of charge carriers from *source* (*S*) to *drain* (*D*) through the *channel* between the *gate* (*G*) elements.

The transistor can be an *n*-channel device (conduction by electrons) or a *p*-channel device (conduction by holes). A discussion of *n*-channel devices applies equally to *p*-channel devices if *complementary* (opposite in sign) voltages and currents are used. Analogies between the JFET and the BJT are shown in Table 5-1. Current and voltage symbology for FETs parallels are given in Table 3-1.

JFET	BJT
source S	emitter E
drain D	collector C
gate G	base B
drain supply V_{DD}	collector supply V_{CC}
gate supply V_{GG}	base supply V_{BB}
drain current i_D	collector current i_C

Table 5-1

The JFET is almost universally applied in the *common-source* (CS) two-port arrangement of Fig. 5-1, where v_{GS} maintains a reverse bias of the gate-source *pn* junction. The resulting gate leakage current is negligibly small for most analyses (usually less than 1 μA), allowing the gate to be treated as an open circuit. Thus, no input characteristic curves are necessary.

Typical *output* or *drain characteristics* for an *n*-channel JFET in CS connection with $v_{GS} \leq 0$ are given in Fig. 5-2(*a*). For a constant value of v_{GS}, the JFET acts as a linear resistive device (in the *ohmic region*) until the *depletion region* of the reverse-biased gate-source junction extends the width of the channel (a condition called *pinchoff*). Above pinchoff but below avalanche breakdown, drain current i_D remains nearly constant

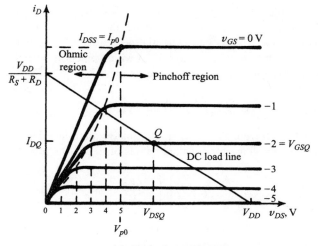

(a) Drain characteristics

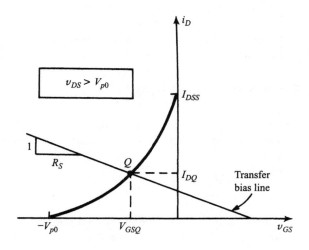

(b) Transfer characteristic

Fig. 5-2 CS n-channel JFET characteristics

as v_{DS} is increased. For specification purposes, the *shorted-gate parameters* I_{DSS} and V_{p0} are defined as indicated in Fig. 5-2(a). Typically, V_{p0} is between 4 and 5 V. As gate potential decreases, the *pinchoff voltage*, that is, the source-to-drain voltage V_p at which pinchoff occurs, also decreases, approximately obeying the equation

$$V_P = V_{p0} + v_{GS} \tag{5.1}$$

The drain current shows an approximate square-law dependence on source-to-gate voltage for constant values of v_{DS} in the pinchoff region

$$i_D = I_{DSS}\left(1 + \frac{v_{GS}}{V_{p0}}\right)^2 \tag{5.2}$$

This accounts for the unequal spacing of the characteristic curves in Fig. 5-2(a). Fig. 5-2(b) is the graph of (5.2), known as the *transfer characteristic* and is utilized in bias determination. The transfer characteristic is also determined by the intersections of the drain characteristics with a fixed vertical line, v_{DS} = constant. To the extent that the drain characteristics actually are horizontal in the pinchoff region, one and the same transfer characteristic will be found for all $v_{DS} > V_{p0}$.

JFET Bias and Load Lines

The commonly used *voltage-divider* bias arrangement of Fig. 5-3(a) can be reduced to its equivalent in Fig. 5-3(b), where the Thévenin parameters are given by

$$R_G = \frac{R_1 R_2}{R_1 + R_2} \quad \text{and} \quad V_{GG} = \frac{R_1}{R_1 + R_2}V_{DD} \tag{5.3}$$

With $i_G = 0$, application of KVL around the gate-source loop of Fig. 5-3(b) yields the equation of the *transfer bias line*,

$$i_D = \frac{V_{GG}}{R_S} - \frac{v_{GS}}{R_S} \tag{5.4}$$

which can be solved simultaneously with (5.2) or plotted on Fig. 5-2(b) to yield I_{DQ} and V_{GSQ}, two of the necessary three quiescent variables.

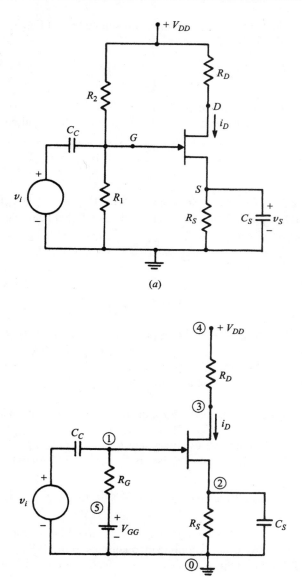

Fig. 5-3 (*a*) JFET biasing circuit; (*b*) equivalent circuit

Application of KVL around the drain-source loop of Fig. 5-3(b) leads to the equation of the *dc load line*,

$$i_D = \frac{V_{DD}}{R_S + R_D} - \frac{v_{DS}}{R_S + R_D} \qquad (5.5)$$

which, when plotted on the drain characteristics of Fig. 5-2(a), yields the remaining quiescent value, V_{DSQ}. Alternatively, with I_{DQ} already determined,

$$V_{DSQ} = V_{DD} - (R_S + R_D)I_{DQ}$$

Example 5.1 In the amplifier of Fig. 5-3(a), $V_{DD} = 20$V, $R_1 = 1$MΩ, $R_2 = 15.7$MΩ, $R_D = 3$kΩ, and $R_S = 2$kΩ. If the JFET characteristics are given by Fig's. 5-4 and 5-5, find (a) I_{DQ}, (b) V_{GSQ}, and (c) V_{DSQ}.

Solution: (a) by (5.3),

$$V_{GG} = \frac{R_1}{R_1 + R_2}V_{DD} = \frac{1 \times 10^6}{16.7 \times 10^6}20 = 1.2\,\text{V}$$

On Fig. 5-4, we construct the transfer bias line (5.4). It intersects the transfer characteristic at the Q point, giving $I_{DQ} = 1.5$ mA.

(b) The Q point of Fig. 5-4 also gives $V_{GSQ} = -2$ V.

(c) We construct the dc load line on the drain characteristics, making use of the v_{DS} intercept of $V_{DD} = 20$ V and the i_D intercept of $V_{DD}/(R_S + R_D)$ = 4mA. The Q point was established at $I_{DQ} = 1.5$ mA in part (a) and at $V_{GSQ} = -2$ V in part (b). Its abscissa is $V_{DSQ} = 12.5$ V. Analytically,

$$V_{DSQ} = V_{DD} - (R_S + R_D)I_{DQ} = 20 - (5 \times 10^3)(1.5 \times 10^{-3}) = 12.5\,\text{V}$$

As is done in BJT circuits (Chapter 3), coupling (or blocking) capacitors are introduced to confine dc quantities to the JFET and its bias circuitry. Further, bypass capacitors C_S effectively remove the gain-reducing source resistor insofar as ac signals are concerned, while allowing R_S to be utilized in favorably setting the gate-source bias voltage. Consequently, an ac load line is introduced with analysis techniques analogous to those of Chapter 3.

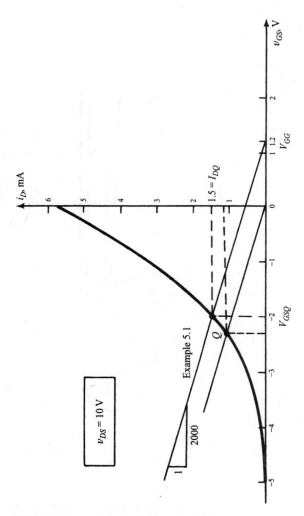

Fig. 5-4 Transfer characteristic for Example 5-1

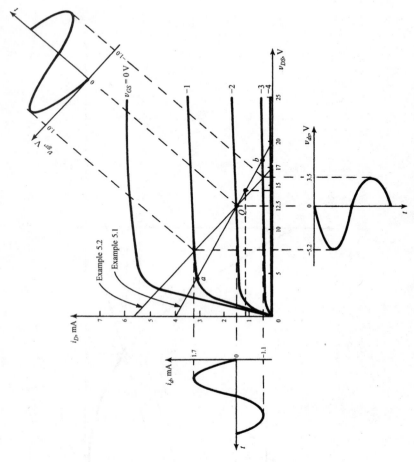

Fig. 5-5 Drain characteristics for Example 5.1

Graphical analysis is favored for large-ac-signal conditions in the JFET, since the square-law relationship between v_{GS} and i_D leads to signal distortion.

Example 5.2 For the amplifier of Example 5.1, let $v_i = \sin t \, \text{V}(\omega = 1 \, \text{rad/s})$ and $C_S \to \infty$. Graphically, determine v_{ds} and i_d.

Solution: Since C_S appears as a short to ac signals, an ac load line must be added to Fig. 5-5, passing through the Q point and intersecting the v_{DS} axis at

$$V_{DSQ} + I_{DQ}R_{ac} = 12.5 + (1.5)(3) = 17 \text{ V}$$

We next construct an auxiliary time axis through Q, perpendicular to the ac load line, for the purpose of showing, on additional auxiliary axes as constructed in Fig. 5-5, the excursions of the i_d and v_{ds} are

$$-1.1 \leq i_d \leq 1.7 \text{ (centered around } I_{DQ} = 1.5 \text{ mA)}$$

$$-5.2 \leq v_{ds} \leq 3.5 \text{ (centered around } V_{DSQ} = 12.5 \text{ V)}$$

as $v_{gs} = v_i$ swings ± 1 V along the ac load line. Note the distortion in the i_d (and also v_{ds}) introduced by the square-law behavior of the JFET characteristics.

MOSFET Construction and Terminal Characteristics

The n-channel MOSFET (Fig. 5-6) has only a single p region (called the *substrate*), one side of which acts as a conducting channel. A metallic gate is separated from the conducting channel by an insulating metal oxide (usually SiO_2), whence the name *insulated-gate* FET (IGFET) for the device. The p-channel MOSFET, formed by interchanging p and n semiconductor materials, is described by complementary voltages and currents.

In an n-channel MOSFET, the gate (positive plate), metal oxide film (dielectric), and substrate (negative plate) form a capacitor, the electric field of which controls channel resistance. When the positive potential of the gate reaches a *threshold voltage* V_T (typically 2 to 4 V), sufficient free electrons are attracted to the region immediately beside the metal oxide film (this is called *enhancement-mode* operation) to induce a conducting channel of low resistivity. If the source-to-drain voltage is increased, the enhanced channel is depleted of free charge carriers in the area near the drain, and pinchoff occurs as in the JFET. Typical drain and transfer characteristics are displayed in Fig. 5-7, where $V_T = 4$ V is used for illustration. Commonly, the manufacturer specifies V_T and a value of pinchoff current I_{Don}. The corresponding value of source-to-gate voltage is V_{GSon}.

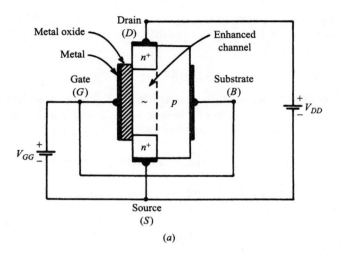

(a)

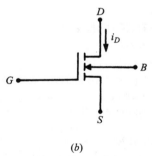

(b)

Fig. 5-6 (a) Construction of an n-channel MOSFET; (b) circuit symbol

The enhancement mode MOSFET, operating in the pinchoff region, is described by (5.1) and (5.2) if V_{p0} and I_{DSS} are replaced with $-V_T$ and I_{Don}, respectively, and if the substrate is shorted to the source, as in Fig. 5-8. Then,

$$i_D = I_{Don}\left(1 - \frac{v_{GS}}{V_T}\right)^2 \qquad (5.6)$$

where $v_{GS} \geq V_T$.

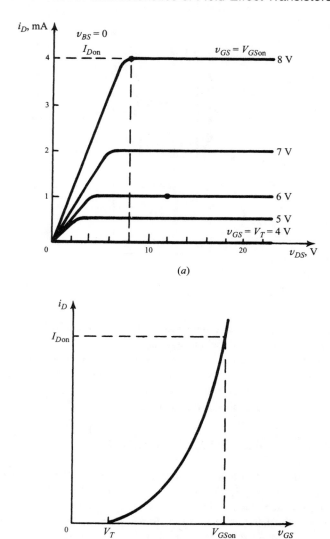

Fig. 5-7 Typical (*a*) drain and (*b*) transfer characteristics of a MOSFET

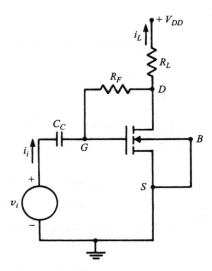

Fig. 5-8 MOSFET with substrate shorted to the source.

Although the enhancement-mode MOSFET is the more popular (it is widely used in digital switching circuits), a *depletion-mode* MOSFET, characterized by a lightly doped channel between heavily doped source and drain electrode areas, is commercially available and can be operated like a JFET. However, that device displays a gate-source input impedance several orders of magnitude smaller than that of the JFET.

MOSFET Bias and Load Lines

Although the transfer characteristic of the MOSFET differs from that of the JFET (compare Fig. 5-2(*b*) with Fig.5-7(*b*)), simultaneous solution with the transfer bias line (5.4) allows determination of the gate-source bias V_{GSQ}. Further, graphical procedures in which dc and ac load lines are constructed on drain characteristics can be utilized with both enhancement-mode and depletion-mode MOSFETs.

The voltage-divider bias arrangement (Fig. 5-3) is readily applicable to the enhancement-mode MOSFET. However, since V_{GSQ} and V_{DSQ} are of the same polarity, *drain-feedback bias*, illustrated in Fig. 5-8, can be utilized to compensate partially for variations in MOSFET characteristics.

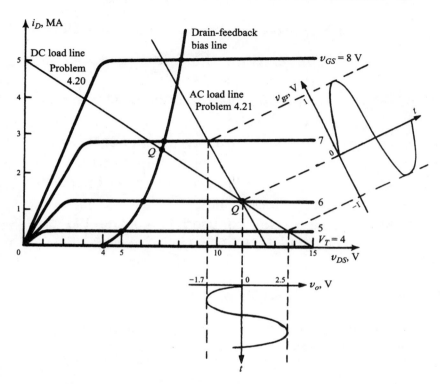

Fig. 5-9 MOSFET drain characteristics for Example 5.3

Example 5.3 In the amplifier of Fig. 5-8, $V_{DD} = 15$ V, $R_L = 3$ kΩ, $R_F = 50$ MΩ. If the MOSFET drain characteristics are given by Fig. 5-9, determine the values of the quiescent quantities.

Solution: The dc load line is constructed on Fig. 5-9 with v_{DS} intercept of $V_{DD} = 15$ V and i_D intercept of $V_{DD}/R_L = 5$ mA. With gate current negligible, no voltage appears across R_F, and so $V_{GS} = V_{DS}$. The *drain-feedback bias line* of Fig. 5-9 is the locus of all points for which $V_{GS} = V_{DS}$. Since the Q point must line on both the dc load line and the drain-feedback bias line, their intersection is the Q point. From Fig. 5-9, $I_{DQ} \approx 2.65$ mA and $V_{DSQ} \approx 6.90$ V.

> # Important Things to Remember
>
> ✔ The three terminals of JFETs and MOSFETs are the gate, drain, and source.
> ✔ The common-source (CS) is the most common connection for FETs.
> ✔ Load line analysis can be used to solve for a FET's voltage and current in a given circuit.
> ✔ The dc biasing determines the quiescent point of operation for the FET.
> ✔ Capacitors can be used to confine the dc quantities to the FET and bias circuitry.

Additional Solved Problems

ASP 5.1 Replace the JFET of Fig. 5-3 with an n-channel enhancement-mode MOSFET characterized by Fig. 5-7. Let $V_{DD} = 16$ V, $V_{GSQ} = 8$ V, $V_{DSQ} = 12$ V, $I_{DQ} = 1$ mA, $R_1 = 5$ MΩ, and $R_2 = 3$ MΩ. Find (a) V_{GG}, (b) R_S, and (c) R_D.

Solution: (a) By (5.3),

$$V_{GG} = R_1 V_{DD} / (R_1 + R_2) = 10 \text{ V}$$

(b) Application of KVL around the smaller gate-source loop of Fig 5-3(b) with $i_G = 0$ leads to

$$R_S = \frac{V_{GG} - V_{GSQ}}{I_{DQ}} = \frac{10 - 8}{1 \times 10^{-3}} = 2 \text{ k}\Omega$$

(c) Using KVL around the drain-source loop of Fig. 5-3(b) and solving for R_D yields

$$R_D = \frac{V_{DD} - V_{DSQ} - I_{DQ}R_S}{I_{DQ}} = \frac{16 - 12 - (1 \times 10^{-3})(2 \times 10^3)}{1 \times 10^{-3}} = 2 \text{k}\Omega$$

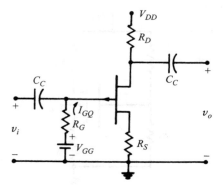

Fig. 5-10 Circuit for ASP 5.2

ASP 5.2 Gate current is negligible for the *p*-channel JFET of Fig. 5-10. If $V_{DD} = 20$ V, $I_{DSS} = -10$ mA, $I_{DQ} = -8$ mA, $V_{p0} = -4$ V, $R_S = 0$, and $R_{D-} = 1.5$ kΩ. Find (*a*) V_{GG}, (*b*) V_{DSQ}.

Solution: (*a*) Solving (5.2) for v_{GS} and substituting Q point conditions yields

$$V_{GSQ} = V_{p0}\left[\left(\frac{I_{DQ}}{I_{DSS}}\right)^{1/2} - 1\right] = -4\left[\left(\frac{-8}{-10}\right)^{1/2} - 1\right] = 0.422 \text{ V}$$

With negligible gate current, KVL requires that

$$V_{GG} = V_{GSQ} = 0.422 \text{ V}.$$

(*b*) Applying KVL around the drain-source loop gives

$$V_{DSQ} = V_{DD} - I_{DQ}R_D = (-20) - (-8 \times 10^{-3})(1.5 \times 10^3) = -8 \text{ V}$$

ASP 5.3 For the *n*-channel enhancement mode MOSFET of Fig. 5-11, gate current is negligible, $I_{Don} = 10$ mA and $V_T = 4$ V. If $R_S = 0$, $R_1 = 50$ kΩ, $V_{DD} = 15$ V, $V_{GSQ} = 3$ V, and $V_{DSQ} = 9$ V, determine the values of (*a*) R_z, and (*b*) R_D.

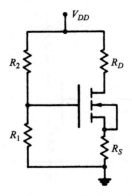

Fig. 5-11 Circuit for ASP 5.3

Solution: Since $i_G = 0$, $V_{GSQ} = V_{GG}$ of (5.3). Solving for R_2 gives

$$R_2 = R_1\left(\frac{V_{DD}}{V_{GSQ}} - 1\right) = 50 \times 10^3\left(\frac{15}{3} - 1\right) = 200 \text{ k}\Omega$$

(b) By (5.6),

$$I_{DQ} = I_{Don}\left(1 - \frac{V_{GSQ}}{V_T}\right)^2 = 10 \times 10^{-3}\left(1 - \frac{3}{4}\right)^2 = 0.625 \text{ mA}$$

Then KVL around the drain-source loop requires that

$$R_D = \frac{V_{DD} - V_{DSQ}}{I_{DQ}} = \frac{15 - 9}{0.625 \times 10^{-3}} = 9.6 \text{ k}\Omega$$

CHAPTER 6
SMALL-SIGNAL MIDFREQUENCY FET AMPLIFIERS

IN THIS CHAPTER:

✔ *Introduction*
✔ *Small-Signal Equivalent Circuits for the FET*
✔ *CS Amplifier Analysis*
✔ *CD Amplifier Analysis*
✔ *CG Amplifier Analysis*

Introduction

Several two-port linear network models are available that allow accurate analysis of the FET for small drain-source voltage and small current excursions about a quiescent point (small-signal operation). In this chapter, all voltage and current signals are considered to be in the midfrequency range, where all capacitors appear as short circuits.

Note!

There are three basic FET amplifier configurations: the *common-source* (CS), *common-drain* (CD) or *source-follower* (SF), and *common-gate* (CG) configurations.

The CS amplifier, which provides good voltage amplification, is most frequently used. The CD and *CG* amplifiers are applied as buffer amplifiers (with high input impedance and near-unity voltage gain) and high-frequency amplifiers, respectively.

Small-Signal Equivalent Circuits for the FET

From FET drain characteristics of Fig. 5-2(a), it is seen that if i_D is taken as the dependent variable, then

$$i_D = f(v_{GS}, v_{DS}) \tag{6.1}$$

For small excursions (ac signals) about the Q point, $\Delta i_D = i_d$. Thus, application of the chain rule to (6.1) leads to

$$i_d = \Delta i_D \approx d i_D = g_m v_{gs} + \frac{1}{r_{ds}} v_{ds} \tag{6.2}$$

where g_m and r_{ds} are defined as follows:

Transconductance $g_m \equiv \left. \dfrac{\partial i_D}{\partial v_{GS}} \right|_Q \approx \left. \dfrac{\Delta i_D}{\Delta v_{GS}} \right|_Q \tag{6.3}$

Source-drain resistance $r_{ds} \equiv \left. \dfrac{\partial v_{DS}}{\partial i_D} \right|_Q \approx \left. \dfrac{\Delta v_{DS}}{\Delta i_D} \right|_Q \tag{6.4}$

As long as the JFET is operated in the pinchoff region, $i_G = i_g = 0$ so that the gate acts as an open circuit. This, along with (6.2), leads to the cur-

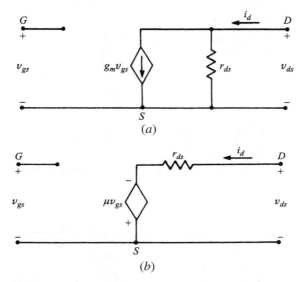

Fig. 6-1 Small-signal models for the CS JFET

rent-source equivalent circuit of Fig. 6-1(a). A voltage-source model is shown in Fig. 6-1(b). Either of these models may be used in analyzing an amplifier but one may be more efficient than the other in a particular circuit.

CS Amplifier Analysis

A simple common-source amplifier is shown in Fig. 6-2(a). Its associated small-signal equivalent model is displayed in Fig. 6-2(b). Source resistor R_S is used to set the Q point but is bypassed by C_S for midfrequency operation.

Example 6.1 In the CS amplifier of Fig. 6-2(b), let $R_D = 3$ kΩ, $\mu = 60$, and $r_{ds} = 30$ kΩ. (a) Find an expression for the voltage-gain ratio $A_v = v_o/v_i$. (b) Evaluate A_v using the given typical values.

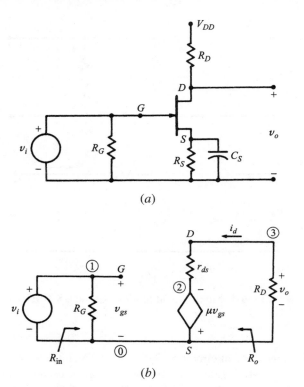

Fig. 6-2 (*a*) CS amplifier; (*b*) Small-signal equivalent circuit

Solution: By voltage division,

$$v_o = -\frac{R_D}{R_D + r_{ds}} \mu v_{gs}$$

Substitution of $v_{gs} = v_i$ and rearrangement gives

$$A_v = \frac{v_o}{v_i} = -\frac{\mu R_D}{R_D + r_{ds}}$$

(*b*) The given values lead to

$$A_v = -\frac{(60)(3 \times 10^3)}{3 \times 10^3 + 30 \times 10^3} = -5.45$$

where the minus sign indicates a 180 degree phase shift between v_i and v_o.

CD Amplifier Analysis

A simple common-drain (or source follower) amplifier is shown in Fig. 6-3(a). Its associated small-signal equivalent circuit is given in Fig. 6-3(b), where the voltage-source equivalent of Fig. 6-1(b) is used to model the FET.

Example 6.2 In the CD amplifier of Fig. 6-3(b), let $R_S = 5$ kΩ, $\mu = 60$, and $r_{ds} = 30$ kΩ. (a) Find an expression for the voltage-gain ratio $A_v = v_o / v_i$. (b) Evaluate A_v using the given typical values.

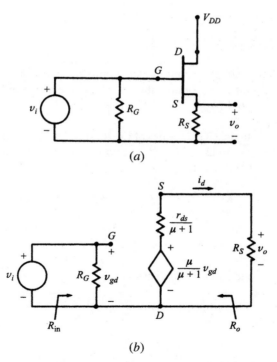

(a)

(b)

Fig. 6-3 (a) CD or SF amplifier; (b) Small-signal equivalent circuit

Solution: (*a*) By voltage division,

$$v_o = \frac{R_S}{R_S + r_{ds}/(\mu+1)} \frac{\mu}{(\mu+1)} v_{gd} = \frac{\mu R_S v_{gd}}{(\mu+1)R_S + r_{ds}}$$

Replacement of v_{gd} by v_i and rearrangement gives

$$A_v = \frac{v_o}{v_i} = \frac{\mu R_S}{(\mu+1)R_S + r_{ds}}$$

(*b*) Substitution of the given values leads to

$$A_v = \frac{(60)(5 \times 10^3)}{(60+1)(5 \times 10^3) + 30 \times 10^3} = 0.895$$

Note that the gain is less than unity. Its positive value indicates that v_o and v_i are in phase.

CG Amplifier Analysis

Fig. 6-4(*a*) is a simple common-gate amplifier circuit. Its small signal equivalent circuit, incorporating the current-source model of Fig. 6-1(*a*), is given in Fig. 6-4(*b*).

Example 6.3 In the CG amplifier of Fig. 6-4(*b*), let $R_D = 1$ kΩ, $g_m = 2 \times 10^{-3}$ S, and $r_{ds} = 30$ kΩ. (*a*) Find an expression for the voltage-gain ratio $A_v = v_o/v_i$. (*b*) Evaluate A_v using the given typical values.

Solution: (*a*) By KCL, $i_i = i_d - g_m v_{gs}$. Applying KVL around the outer loop gives

$$v_o = (i_d - g_m v_{gs})r_{ds} - v_{gs}$$

But, $v_{gs} = -v_i$ and $i_d = -v_o/R_D$. Thus,

$$v_o = \left(-\frac{v_o}{R_D} + g_m v_i\right)r_{ds} + v_i$$

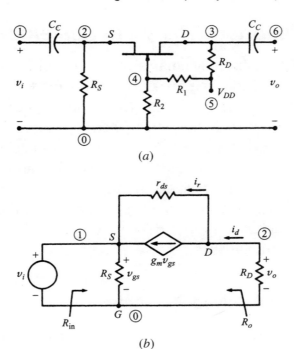

Fig. 6-4 (a) CG amplifier; (b) CG small-signal equivalent circuit

and

$$A_v = \frac{v_o}{v_i} = \frac{(g_m r_{ds} + 1)R_D}{R_D + r_{ds}}$$

(b) Substitution of the given values yields

$$A_v = \frac{(61)(1 \times 10^3)}{1 \times 10^3 + 30 \times 10^3} = 1.97$$

Important Things to Remember

✔ For sufficiently small signals, the JFET can be analyzed using two-port network models.
✔ The common-source (CS) amplifier configuration is most frequently used.
✔ Common-drain (CD) and common-gate (CG) amplifiers are mostly used as buffers and high-frequency amplifiers, respectively.
✔ The transconductance g_m and the source-drain resistance r_{ds} are derived from the FET drain characteristics.

Additional Solved Problems

ASP 6.1 (*a*) For the JFET amplifier of Example 5.1, use the drain characteristics of Fig. 5-5 to determine the small-signal equivalent-circuit constants g_m and r_{ds}. (*b*) Alternatively, evaluate g_m from the transfer characteristic.

Solution: (*a*) Let v_{gs} change by ± 1 V about the Q point. Then, by (6.3),

$$g_m \approx \left. \frac{\Delta i_D}{\Delta v_{gs}} \right|_Q = \frac{(3.3 - 0.3) \times 10^{-3}}{2} = 1.5 \text{ mS}$$

At the Q point of Fig. 5-5(*b*), while v_{DS} changes from 5 V to 20 V, i_D changes from 1.4 mA to 1.6 mA. Thus, by (6.4),

$$r_{ds} \approx \left. \frac{\Delta v_{DS}}{\Delta i_D} \right|_Q = \frac{20 - 5}{(1.6 - 1.4) \times 10^{-3}} = 75 \text{ k}\Omega$$

(*b*) At the Q point of Fig. 5-5(*a*), while i_D changes from 1 mA to 2 mA, v_{GS} changes from -2.4 V to -1.75 V. By (6.3),

$$g_m \approx \frac{\Delta i_D}{\Delta v_{GS}}\bigg|_Q = \frac{(2-1)\times 10^{-3}}{-1.75-(-2.4)} = 1.54 \text{ mS}$$

ASP 6.2 For the JFET amplifier of Fig. 6-5, $g_m = 2$ mS, $r_{ds} = 30$ kΩ, $R_S = 3$ kΩ, $R_D = R_L = 2$ kΩ, $R_G = 160$ kΩ, $R_1 = 200$ kΩ, $R_2 = 800$ kΩ, and $r_i = 5$ kΩ. Assume C_C is large and C_S is removed from the circuit, all else remaining the same. Find (a) the voltage gain ratio $A_v = v_L/v_i$, and (b) the current-gain ratio $A_i = i_L/i_i$.

Solution: The voltage-source small-signal model is given in Fig. 6-6. Voltage division and KVL give

$$v_{gs} = \frac{R_G}{R_G + r_i} v_i - i_d R_S \tag{A.1}$$

But, by Ohm's law,

$$i_d = \frac{\mu v_{gs}}{r_{ds} + R_S + R_D \parallel R_L} \tag{A.2}$$

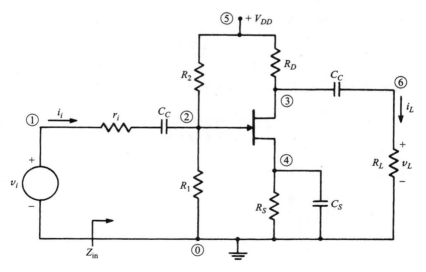

Fig. 6-5 Circuit for ASP 6.2

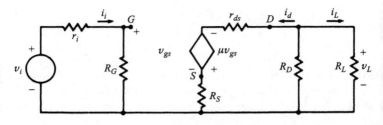

Fig. 6-6 Small-signal equivalent

Substituting (A.2) into (A.1) and solving for v_{gs} yields

$$v_{gs} = \frac{R_G(r_{ds} + R_S + R_D \parallel R_L)}{(R_G + r_i)[r_{ds} + (\mu + 1)R_S + R_D \parallel R_L]} v_i \tag{A.3}$$

Now voltage division gives

$$v_L = -\frac{R_D \parallel R_L}{r_{ds} + R_S + R_D \parallel R_L} \mu v_{gs} \tag{A.4}$$

and substitution of (A.3) into (A.4) and rearrangement gives

$$A_v = \frac{v_L}{v_i} = \frac{-\mu R_G R_D R_L}{(R_G + r_i)\{(R_D + R_L)[r_{ds} + (\mu + 1)R_S] + R_D R_L\}} \tag{A.5}$$

With $\mu = g_m r_{ds}$ and the given values, (A.5) becomes

$$A_v = \frac{-(2 \times 10^{-3})(160)(2)(2)}{(160 + 5)\{(2 + 2)[30 + (60 + 1)3] + (2)(2)\}} = -0.272$$

(*b*) The current gain is found as

$$A_i = \frac{i_L}{i_i} = \frac{v_L / R_L}{v_i(R_G + r_i)} = \frac{A_v(R_G + r_i)}{R_L} = \frac{(-0.272)(160 + 5)}{2} = -22.4$$

Chapter 7

FREQUENCY EFFECTS IN AMPLIFIERS

Introduction

In the analyses of the BJT and FET amplifiers, we assumed operation in the midfrequency range in which the reactances of all bypass and coupling capacitors can be considered to be zero while all inherent capacitive reactances associated with transistors are infi-

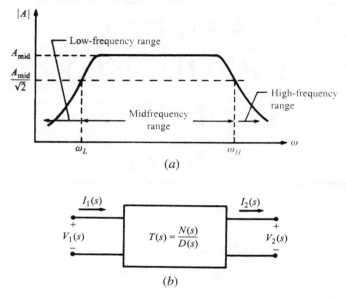

Fig. 7-1 (*a*) Band-pass amplifier response; (*b*) two-port model

nitely large. However, over a wide range of signal frequencies, the response is that of a *band-pass filter*. Low and high frequencies are attenuated but signals over a band (or range) of frequencies between high and low are not attenuated.

Fig. 7-1(a) illustrates the typical frequency behavior of an RC-coupled amplifier. In practical amplifiers, the midfrequency range spans several orders of magnitude so that terms in the gain ratio expression that alter low-frequency gain are essentially constant over the high-frequency range. Conversely, terms that alter high-frequency gain are practically constant over the low-frequency range. Thus the high- and low-frequency analyses of amplifiers are treated as two independent problems.

Bode Plots and Frequency Response

Any linear two-port electrical network that is free of independent sources (including small-signal amplifier equivalent circuits) can be reduced to the form of Fig. 7-1(*b*), where $T(s) = N(s)/D(s)$ is the Laplace-domain *transfer function* (a ratio of port variables).

Of particular interest in amplifier analysis are the *current-gain ratio* (*transfer function*) $T(s) = A_i(s)$ and *voltage-gain ratio* (*transfer function*) $T(s) = A_v(s)$. For a sinusoidal input voltage signal, the Laplace transform pair

$$v_1(t) = V_{1m} \sin \omega t \leftrightarrow V_1(s) = \frac{V_{1m}\omega}{s^2 + \omega^2}$$

is applicable and the network response is given by

$$V_2(s) = \frac{A_v(s)V_{1m}\omega}{s^2 + \omega^2} \tag{7.1}$$

Without loss of generality, we may assume that the polynomial $D(s) = 0$ has n distinct roots. Then the partial-fraction expansion of (7.1) yields

$$V_2(s) = \frac{k_1}{s - j\omega} + \frac{k_2}{s + j\omega} + \frac{k_3}{s + p_1} + \frac{k_4}{s + p_2} + \ldots + \frac{k_{n+2}}{s + p_n} \tag{7.2}$$

where the first two terms on the right-hand side are forced-response terms (called the *frequency response*) and the balance of the terms constitute the *transient response*. The transient response diminishes to zero with time, provided the roots of $D(s) = 0$ are located in the left half plane of complex numbers (the condition for a *stable* system).

The coefficients k_1 and k_2 are evaluated by the method of residues, and the results are used in an inverse transformation to the time-domain steady-state sinusoidal response given by

$$v_2(t) = V_{1m} \, | A_v(j\omega) | \sin(\omega t + \phi) = V_{2m} \sin(\omega t + \phi) \tag{7.3}$$

The *network phase angle* ϕ is defined as

$$\phi = \tan^{-1} \frac{\text{Im}\{A_v(j\omega)\}}{\text{Re}\{A_v(j\omega)\}} \tag{7.4}$$

From (7.4), it is apparent that a sinusoidal input to a stable, linear, two-port network results in a steady-state output that is also sinusoidal. The input and output waveforms differ only in amplitude and phase angle.

For convenience, we make the following definitions:

1. Call $A(j\omega)$ the *frequency transfer function*.
2. Define $M \equiv |A(j\omega)|$, the *gain ratio*.
3. Define $M_{db} \equiv 20 \log M = 20\log|A(j\omega)|$, the *amplitude ratio*, measured in *decibels* (dB).

The subscript v or i may be added to any of these quantities to specifically denote reference to voltage or current, respectively. The graph of M_{db} (simultaneously with ϕ if desired) versus the logarithm of the input signal frequency (positive values only) is called a *Bode plot*.

Example 7.1 A simple first-order network has Laplace-domain transfer function and frequency transfer function

$$A(s) = \frac{1}{\tau s + 1} \qquad \text{and} \qquad A(j\omega) = \frac{1}{j\omega\tau + 1}$$

where τ is the system time constant. (*a*) Determine the network phase angle ϕ and the amplitude ratio M_{db} and (*b*) construct the Bode plot for the network.

Solution: (*a*) In polar form, the given frequency transfer function is

$$A(j\omega) = \frac{1}{\sqrt{1 + (\omega\tau)^2}} \angle - \tan^{-1}(\omega\tau)$$

Hence,

$$\phi = -\tan^{-1}(\omega\tau) \tag{7.5}$$

and

$$M_{db} = 20 \log |A(j\omega)| = 20 \log \frac{1}{\sqrt{1 + (\omega\tau)^2}} = -10 \log[1 + (\omega\tau)^2] \tag{7.6}$$

(*b*) If values of (7.5) and (7.6) are calculated and plotted for various values of ω, then a Bode plot is generated. This is done in Fig. 7-2, where ω is given in terms of time constants τ rather than, say, hertz. This particular system is called a *lag network* because its phase angle ϕ is negative for all ω.

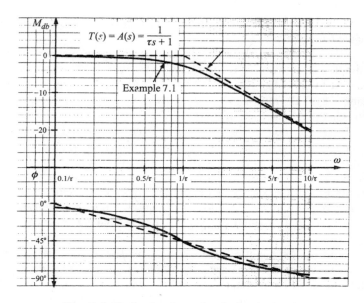

Fig. 7-2 Bode plot for a simple lag network

Example 7.2 A simple first-order network has Laplace-domain transfer function and frequency transfer function

$$A(s) = \tau s + 1 \quad \text{and} \quad A(j\omega) = j\omega\tau + 1$$

Determine the network phase angle ϕ and the amplitude ratio M_{db}, and discuss the nature of the Bode plot.

Solution: After $A(j\omega)$ is converted to polar form, it becomes apparent that

$$\phi = \tan^{-1}(\omega\tau) \tag{7.7}$$

and

$$M_{db} = 20\log|A(j\omega)| = 20\log\sqrt{1+(\omega\tau)^2} = 10\log[1+(\omega\tau)^2] \tag{7.8}$$

Comparison of (7.5) and (7.7) reveals that the network phase angle is the mirror image of the phase angle for the network of Ex. 7.1. Further, (7.8) shows that the amplitude ratio is the mirror image of the amplitude ratio of Ex. 7.1. Since here the phase angle everywhere is positive, the network is called a *lead network*.

A *break frequency* or *corner frequency* is the frequency $\omega = 1/\tau$. For a simple lag network, it is the frequency at which $M^2 = |A(j\omega)|^2$ has changed by 50% from its value at $\omega = 0$. At that frequency, M_{db} has changed by 3 dB from its value at $\omega = 0$. Corner frequencies serve as key points in the construction of Bode plots.

The exact Bode plot of a network transfer function is tedious to construct. Frequently, sufficiently accurate information can be obtained from an *asymptotic* Bode plot.

Example 7.3 The exact Bode plot for the first-order system of Example 7.1 is given in Fig. 7.2. (*a*) Add the asymptotic Bode plot; (*b*) Describe the asymptotic Bode plot for the system of Example 7.2.

Solution: (*a*) Asymptotic Bode plots are piecewise-linear approximations. The asymptotic plot of M_{db} for a simple lag network has value zero out to the single break frequency $\omega = 1/\tau$ and then *decreases* at 20 dB per decade. The asymptotic plot of ϕ has the value zero out to $\omega = 1/\tau$, *decreases* linearly to $-90°$ at $\omega = 10/\tau$, and then is constant at $-90°$. Both asymptotic plots are shown dashed in Fig. 7-2.

(*b*) The asymptotic Bode plot for a simple lead network is the mirror image of that for a simple lag network. Thus, the asymptotic plot of M_{db} is zero out to $\omega = 1/\tau$ and then *increases* at 20 dB per decade. The plot of ϕ has the value zero out to $\omega = 0.1/\tau$, and *increases* linearly to $90°$ at $\omega = 1/\tau$, and then remains constant at $90°$.

Low-Frequency Effects of Bypass Coupling Capacitors

As the frequency of the input signal to an amplifier decreases below the midfrequency range, the voltage (or current) gain ratio decreases in magnitude. The *low-frequency cutoff point* ω_L is the frequency at which the gain ratio equals $1/\sqrt{2}$ (=0.707) times its midfrequency value (Fig. 7-1(*a*)), or at which M_{db} has decreased by exactly 3 dB from its midfrequency value. The range of frequencies below ω_L is called the *low-frequency region*. Low-frequency amplifier performance (attenuation, really) is a consequence of the use of bypass and coupling capacitors to fashion the dc bias characteristics. When viewed from the low-frequency region, such amplifier response is analogous to that of a *high-pass filter* (signals for which $\omega < \omega_L$ are appreciably attenuated, whereas higher-frequency signals with $\omega \geq \omega_L$ are unattenuated).

Example 7.4 For the amplifier of Fig. 3-7, assume that $C_C \to \infty$ but that the bypass capacitor C_E cannot be neglected. Also, let $h_{re} = h_{re} \approx 0$ and $R_i = 0$. Find an expression that is valid for small signals and that gives (*a*) the voltage-gain ratio $A_v(s)$ at any frequency. Then find (*b*) the voltage-gain ratio at low frequencies, (*c*) the voltage-gain at high frequencies, and (*d*) the low-frequency cutoff point. (*e*) Sketch the asymptotic Bode plot for the amplifier (amplitude ratio only).

Solution: (*a*) The small-signal low-frequency equivalent circuit (with the approximation implemented) is displayed in Fig. 7-3.

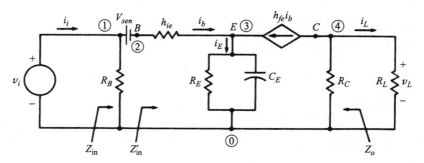

Fig. 7-3 Low-frequency equivalent circuit

In the Laplace domain, we have

$$Z_E = R_E \parallel \frac{1}{sC_E} = \frac{(R_E)(1/sC_E)}{R_E + 1/sC_E} = \frac{R_E}{sR_EC_E + 1}$$

We next note that

$$I_E = I_b + h_{fe}I_b = (h_{fe} + 1)I_b \tag{7.9}$$

Then, KVL and (7.9) yield

$$V_i = h_{ie}I_b + Z_E I_E = [h_{ie} + (h_{fe} + 1)Z_E]I_b \qquad (7.10)$$

But, by Ohm's law,

$$V_L = -(h_{fe}I_b)(R_C \parallel R_L) = -\frac{h_{fe}R_C R_L}{R_C + R_L}I_b \qquad (7.11)$$

Solving (7.10) for I_b, substituting the rest into (7.11), and rearranging gives the desired voltage-gain ratio

$$A_v(s) = \frac{V_L}{V_i} = -\frac{h_{fe}R_C R_L}{R_C + R_L}\frac{sR_E C_E + 1}{sR_E C_E h_{ie} + h_{ie} + (h_{fe} + 1)R_E} \qquad (7.12)$$

(b) The low-frequency voltage-gain ratio is obtained by letting $s \to 0$ in (7.12):

$$A_v(0) = \lim_{s \to 0}\frac{V_L}{V_i} = -\frac{h_{fe}R_C R_L}{(R_C + R_L)(h_{ie} + (h_{fe} + 1)R_E)} \qquad (7.13)$$

(c) The higher-frequency (midfrequency) voltage-gain ratio is obtained by letting $s \to \infty$ in (7.12):

$$A_v(\infty) = \lim_{s \to \infty}\frac{V_L}{V_i} = -\frac{h_{fe}R_C R_L}{R_C + R_L}\frac{R_E C_E + 1/s}{R_E C_E h_{ie} + [h_{ie} + (h_{fe} + 1)R_E]/s}$$
$$= -\frac{h_{fe}R_C R_L}{h_{ie}(R_C + R_L)} \qquad (7.14)$$

(d) Equation (7.12) can be rearranged to give

$$A_v(s) = -\frac{h_{fe}R_C R_L}{(R_C + R_L)[h_{ie} + (h_{fe} + 1)R_E]}\frac{sR_E C_E + 1}{s\dfrac{R_E C_E h_{ie}}{[h_{ie} + (h_{fe} + 1)R_E]} + 1} \qquad (7.15)$$

which is clearly of the form

$$A_v(s) = k_v \frac{\tau_1 s + 1}{\tau_2 s + 1}$$

Thus, we may use (7.15) to write

$$\omega_1 = \frac{1}{\tau_1} = \frac{1}{C_E R_E} \qquad (7.16)$$

and

$$\omega_2 = \frac{1}{\tau_2} = \frac{h_{ie} + (h_{fe} + 1)R_E}{C_E R_E h_{ie}} \tag{7.17}$$

Typically, $h_{fe} \gg 1$ and $h_{fe}R_E \gg h_{ie}$, so a reasonable approximation of ω_2 is

$$\omega_2 \approx \frac{1}{C_E h_{ie} / h_{fe}} \tag{7.18}$$

Since h_{ie}/h_{fe} is typically an order of magnitude smaller than R_E, ω_2 is an order of magnitude greater than ω_1, and $\omega_L = \omega_2$.

(e) The low- and midfrequency asymptotic Bode plot is depicted in Fig. 7-4, where ω_1 and ω_2 are given by (7.16) and (7.18), respectively. From (7.13) and (7.14),

$$M_{dbL} = 20 \log \frac{h_{fe} R_C R_L}{(R_C + R_L)(h_{ie} + (h_{fe} + 1)R_E)}$$

and

$$M_{dbM} = 20 \log \frac{h_{fe} R_C R_L}{h_{ie}(R_C + R_L)}$$

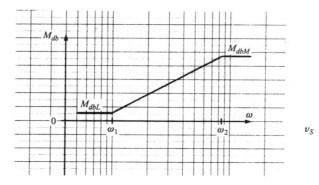

Fig. 7-4 Bode plot for Example 7.4(e)

High-Frequency Hybrid-π BJT Model

Because of capacitance that is inherent within the transistor, amplifier current- and voltage-gain ratios decrease in magnitude as the frequency of the input signal increases beyond the midfrequency range. The *high-frequency cutoff point* ω_H is the frequency at which the gain ratio equals $1/\sqrt{2}$ times its midfrequency value (see Fig. 7-1(a)), or at which M_{db} has decreased by 3 dB from its midfrequency value. The range of frequencies above ω_H is called the *high-frequency region*. Like ω_L, ω_H is a break frequency.

The most useful high-frequency model for the BJT is called the *hybrid-π equivalent circuit* (see Fig. 7-5). In this model, the reverse voltage ratio h_{re} and output admittance h_{oe} are assumed negligible. The *base ohmic resistance* $r_{bb'}$ assumed to be located between the base terminal B and the base junction B', has a constant value (typically 10 to 50 Ω) that depends directly on the base width. The *base-emitter junction resistance* $r_{b'e}$ is usually much larger than $r_{bb'}$ and can be calculated as

$$r_{b'e} = \frac{V_T(\beta+1)}{I_{EQ}} = \frac{V_T \beta}{I_{CQ}}$$

Capacitance C_μ is the depletion capacitance associated with the reverse-biased collector-base junction. Its value is a function of V_{BCQ}. Capacitance $C_\pi (>>C_\mu)$ is the diffusion capacitance associated with the forward-biased base-emitter junction. Its value is a function of I_{EQ}.

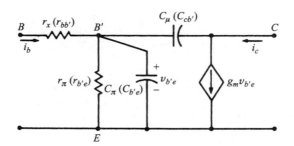

Fig. 7-5 Hybrid-π model for the BJT

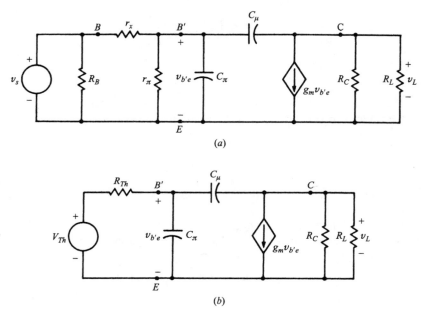

(a)

(b)

Fig. 7-6 Hybrid-π model for the amplifier of Ex. 7.5

Example 7.5 Apply the hybrid-π model of Fig. 7-5 to the amplifier of Fig. 3-7 to find an expression for its voltage-gain ratio $A_v(s)$ valid at high frequencies. Assume $R_i = 0$.

Solution: The high-frequency hybrid-π, small-signal equivalent circuit is drawn in Fig. 7-6(a). To simplify the analysis, a Thévenin equivalent circuit may be found for the network to the left of terminal pair $B'E$, with

$$V_{Th} = \frac{r_\pi}{r_\pi + r_x} v_s \qquad (7.19)$$

and

$$R_{Th} = r_\pi \parallel r_x = \frac{r_\pi r_x}{r_\pi + r_x} \qquad (7.20)$$

Figure 7-6(b) shows the circuit with the Thévenin equivalent in position. Using $v_{b'e}$ and v_L as node voltages and working in the Laplace domain, we may write the following two equations:

$$\frac{V_{b'e} - V_{Th}}{R_{Th}} + \frac{V_{b'e}}{1/sC_\pi} + \frac{V_{b'e} - V_L}{1/sC_\mu} = 0 \qquad (7.21)$$

$$\frac{V_L}{R_C \parallel R_L} + g_m V_{b'e} + \frac{V_L - V_{b'e}}{1/sC_\mu} = 0 \qquad (7.22)$$

The latter equation can be solved for $V_{b'e}$, then substituted into (7.21) and the result rearranged to give the voltage ratio V_{Th}/V_L:

$$\frac{V_{Th}}{V_L} = \frac{s^2 C_\mu C_\pi R_{Th}(R_C \parallel R_L) + s[(1 - g_m)C_\mu(R_C \parallel R_L)] + 1}{(R_C \parallel R_L)(sC_\mu - g_m)} \qquad (7.23)$$

For typical values, the coefficient of s^2 on the right side of (7.23) is several orders of magnitude smaller than the other terms. By approximating this coefficient as zero (i.e., neglecting the s^2-term), we neglect a breakpoint at a frequency much greater than ω_H. Doing so and using (7.19), we obtain the desired high-frequency voltage-gain ratio

$$A_v(s) = \frac{V_L}{V_S} = \frac{r_\pi}{r_\pi + r_x} \frac{(R_C \parallel R_L)(sC_\mu - g_m)}{s[(1 - g_m)C_\mu(R_C \parallel R_L)] + 1}$$

High-Frequency FET Models

The small-signal, high-frequency model for the FET is an extension of the midfrequency model of Fig. 6-1. Three capacitors are added: C_{gs} between gate and source, C_{gd} between gate and drain, and C_{ds} between the drain and source. They are all of the same order of magnitude—typically 1–10 pF. Fig. 7-7 shows the small-signal, high-frequency model based on the current-source model of Fig. 6-1(a). Another model, based on the voltage-source model of Fig. 6-1(b), can also be drawn.

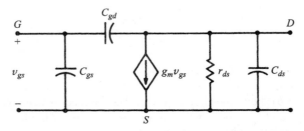

Fig. 7-7 High-frequency, small-signal current-source FET model

Example 7.6 For the JFET amplifier of Fig. 5-3(b), (a) find an expression for the high-frequency voltage-gain ratio $A_v(s)$ and (b) determine the high-frequency cutoff point.

Solution: (a) The high-frequency, small-signal equivalent circuit is displayed in Fig. 7-8, which incorporates Fig. 7-7. We first find a Thévenin equivalent for the network to the left of terminal pair a,a'.

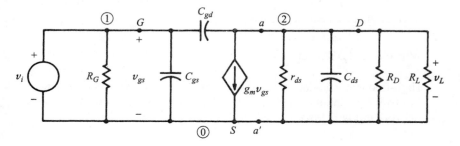

Fig. 7-8 High-frequency JFET amplifier for Ex. 7.6

Noting that $v_{gs} = v_i$, we see that the open-circuit voltage is given by

$$V_{Th} = v_i - \frac{g_m}{sC_{gd}} v_i = \frac{sC_{gd} - g_m}{sC_{gd}} v_i$$

If v_i is deactivated, $v_i = v_{gs} = 0$ and the dependent current source is zero (open-circuited). A driving-point source connected to a,a' sees only

$$Z_{Th} = \frac{v_{dp}}{i_{dp}} = \frac{1}{sC_{gd}}$$

Now, with the Thévenin equivalent in place, voltage division leads to

$$v_L = \frac{Z_{eq}}{Z_{eq} + Z_{Th}} V_{Th} = \frac{1}{1 + Z_{Th}/Z_{eq}} \frac{sC_{gd} - g_m}{sC_{gd}} v_i \qquad (7.24)$$

where

$$\frac{1}{Z_{eq}} = Y_{eq} = sC_{ds} + \frac{1}{r_{ds}} + \frac{1}{R_D} + \frac{1}{R_L} = sC_{ds} + g_{ds} + G_D + G_L \qquad (7.25)$$

Rearranging (7.24) and using (7.25), we get

$$A_v(s) = \frac{v_L}{v_i} = \frac{sC_{gd} - g_m}{s(C_{ds} + C_{gd}) + g_{ds} + G_D + G_L} \tag{7.26}$$

(b) From (7.26), the high-frequency cutoff point is obviously

$$\omega_H = \frac{g_{ds} + G_D + G_L}{C_{ds} + C_{gd}}$$

Note that the high-frequency cutoff point is independent of C_{gs} if source internal impedance is negligible.

Miller Capacitance

High-frequency models of transistors characteristically include a capacitor path from input to output, modeled as admittance Y_F in the two-port network of Fig. 7-9(a).

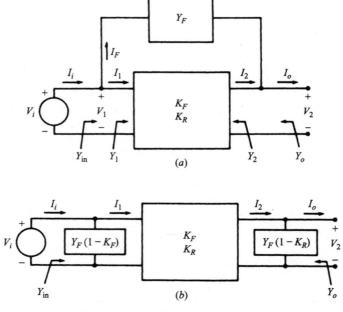

Fig. 7-9 Two-port network models for Miller capacitance

This added conduction path generally increases the difficulty of analysis. We would like to replace it with an equivalent shunt element. Referring to Fig. 7-9(*a*) and using KCL, we have

$$Y_{in} = \frac{I_i}{V_1} = \frac{I_1 + I_F}{V_1} \qquad (7.27)$$

But,

$$I_F = (V_1 - V_2)Y_F \qquad (7.28)$$

Substitution of (7.28) into (7.27) gives

$$Y_{in} = \frac{I_1}{V_1} + \frac{(V_1 - V_2)Y_F}{V_1} = Y_1 + (1 - K_F)Y_F \qquad (7.29)$$

where $K_F = V_2/V_1$ is obviously the forward voltage-gain ratio of the amplifier.

In a similar manner,

$$Y_o = \frac{-I_o}{V_2} = \frac{-(I_2 + I_F)}{V_2} \qquad (7.30)$$

and the use of (7.28) in (7.30) gives us

$$Y_o = -\left(\frac{I_2}{V_2} + \frac{(V_1 - V_2)Y_F}{V_2} \right) = -[-Y_2 + (K_R - 1)Y_F] = Y_2 + (1 - K_R)Y_F$$

$$(7.31)$$

where $K_R = V_1/V_2$ is reverse voltage-gain ratio of the amplifier.

Equations (7.29) and (7.31) suggest that the feedback admittance Y_F can be replaced with two shunt-connected admittances as shown in Fig. 7-9(*b*). When this two-port network is used to model an amplifier, the voltage gain K_F usually turns out to have a large negative value, so that $(1 - K_F)Y_F \approx |K_F|Y_F$.

 **Note!**

Hence, a small feedback capacitance appears as a large shunt capacitance called the *Miller capacitance*.

On the other hand, K_R is typically small so that $(1 - K_R)Y_F \approx Y_F$.

Important Things to Remember

✔ The actual response of an amplifier circuit is that of a band-pass filter

✔ The roll-off of the response at lower frequencies is primarily due to the coupling and bypass capacitors

✔ The roll-off of the response at higher frequencies is primarily due to the inherent internal capacitances of the various pn junctions

---

Additional Solved Problems

ASP 7.1 Sketch the asymptotic Bode plot (M_{db} only) associated with the output-to-input voltage ratio of the circuit in Fig. 7-10.

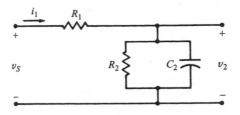

Fig. 7-10 Circuit for ASP 7.1

Solution: By voltage division,

$$V_2 = \frac{R_2 \parallel (1/sC_2)}{R_1 + R_2 + 1/sC_2} V_S = \frac{\dfrac{R_2}{sR_2C_2 + 1}}{R_1 + \dfrac{R_2}{sR_2C_2 + 1}} V_S$$

and the Laplace-domain transfer function is

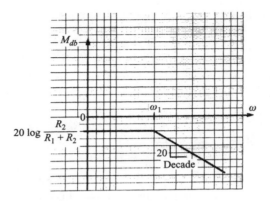

Fig. 7-11 Bode plot for ASP 7.1

$$T(s) = \frac{V_2}{V_S} = \frac{R_2/(R_1+R_2)}{s\left(\dfrac{R_1R_2}{R_1+R_2}\right)C_2+1} = \frac{K_b}{sR_{eq}C_2+1}$$

From $T(s)$, it is apparent that the circuit forms a low-pass filter with low-frequency gain $T(0) = R_2/(R_1+R_2)$ and a corner frequency $\omega_1 = 1/\tau_1 = 1/R_{eq}C_2$. Its Bode plot is shown in Fig. 7-11.

ASP 7.2 The small-signal equivalent of a common-emitter BJT amplifier is shown in Fig. 7-3. The bypass capacitor C_E cannot be neglected. Find expressions for the (a) current-gain ratio $A_i(s)$, (b) the current-gain ratio at low frequencies and (c) The midfrequency current-gain ratio.

Solution: (a) By current division for Laplace-domain quantities,

$$I_b = \frac{R_B}{R_B + h_{ie} + Z_E} I_i \tag{A.1}$$

where

$$Z_E = R_E \parallel \frac{1}{sC_E} = \frac{R_E}{sC_ER_E+1} \tag{A.2}$$

Also,

$$I_L = \frac{-R_C}{R_C + R_L} h_{fe} I_b \tag{A.3}$$

Substitution of (A.1) into (A.3) gives the current gain ratio as

$$A_i = \frac{I_L}{I_i} = \frac{-R_C}{R_C + R_L} \frac{h_{fe} R_B}{R_B + h_{ie} + Z_E} \tag{A.4}$$

Using (A.2) in (A.4) and rearranging leads to the desired current-gain ratio

$$A_i(s) = \frac{\dfrac{-h_{fe} R_C R_B}{(R_C + R_L)(R_E + h_{ie} + R_B)}(sR_E C_E + 1)}{s\dfrac{R_E C_E(h_{ie} + R_B)}{(R_E + h_{ie} + R_B)} + 1} \tag{A-5}$$

(b) The low-frequency current-gain ratio is obtained by letting $s \to 0$ in (A.5):

$$A_i(0) = \lim_{s \to 0} \frac{I_L}{I_i} = \frac{-h_{fe} R_C R_B}{(R_C + R_L)(R_E + h_{ie} + R_B)}$$

(c) The midfrequency current-gain ratio is obtained by letting $s \to \infty$ in (A.5):

$$A_i(\infty) = \lim_{s \to \infty} \frac{I_L}{I_i} = \frac{-h_{fe} R_C R_B}{(R_C + R_L)(h_{ie} + R_B)}$$

Chapter 8
OPERATIONAL AMPLIFIERS

IN THIS CHAPTER:

✔ *Introduction*
✔ *Ideal and Practical Op Amps*
✔ *Op Amp Circuits*

Introduction

The name *operational amplifier* (op amp) was originally given to an amplifier that could be easily modified by external circuitry to perform mathematical operations (addition, scaling, integration, etc.) in analog-computer applications. However, with the advent of solid-state technology, op amps have become highly reliable, miniaturized, temperature-stabilized, and consistently predictable in performance. They now figure as fundamental building blocks in basic amplification and signal conditioning, in active filters, function generators, and switching circuits.

Ideal and Practical Op Amps

An op amp amplifies the difference $v_d \equiv v_1 - v_2$ between two input signals (see Fig. 8-1), exhibiting the open-loop voltage gain

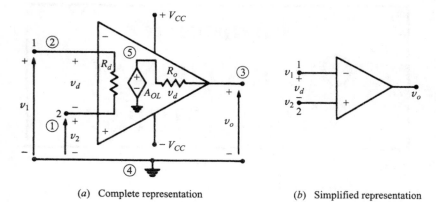

(a) Complete representation   (b) Simplified representation

Fig. 8-1 Operational amplifier

$$A_{OL} = \frac{v_o}{v_d} \tag{8.1}$$

In Fig. 8-1, terminal 1 is the *inverting input* (labeled with a minus sign on the actual amplifier). Signal v_1 is amplified in magnitude and appears phase-inverted at the output. Terminal 2 is the *noninverting input* (labeled with a plus sign). The output due to v_2 is phase-preserved.

In magnitude, the open-loop voltage gain in op amps ranges from 10^4 to 10^7. The maximum magnitude of the output voltage from an op amp is called its *saturation voltage*. This voltage is approximately 2 V smaller than the power supply voltage. In other words, the amplifier is linear over the range

$$-(V_{CC} - 2) < v_o < V_{CC} - 2 \ \text{V}$$

The ideal op amp has three essential characteristics that serve as standards for assessing the goodness of a *practical op amp*:

1. The open-loop gain A_{OL} is negatively infinite.
2. The input impedance R_d between terminals 1 and 2 is infinitely large. Thus, the input current is zero.
3. The output impedance R_o is zero. Consequently, the output voltage is independent of the load.

Fig. 8-1(a) models the practical characteristics.

Example 8.1 An op amp has saturation voltage V_{osat} = 10 V, an open-loop voltage gain of -10^5, and input impedance of 100 kΩ. Find (a) the value of v_d that will just drive the amplifier to saturation and (b) the op amp input current at the onset of saturation.

Solution: (a) By (8.1),

$$v_d = \frac{\pm V_{out}}{A_{OL}} = \frac{\pm 10}{-10^5} = \pm 0.1 \text{ mV}$$

(b) Let i_{in} be the current into terminal 1 of Fig. 8-1(b). Then,

$$i_{in} = \frac{v_d}{R_d} = \frac{\pm 0.1 \times 10^{-3}}{100 \times 10^3} = \pm 1 \text{ nA}$$

In application, a large percentage of negative feedback is used with the operational amplifier, giving a circuit whose characteristics depend almost entirely on circuit elements external to the basic op amp. The error due to treatment of the basic op amp as ideal tends to diminish in the presence of negative feedback.

Op Amp Circuits

The *inverting amplifier* of Fig. 8-2 has its noninverting input connected to ground or common. A signal is applied through input resistor R_1, and negative current feedback is implemented through *feedback resistor R_F*. Output v_o has polarity opposite that of input v_S.

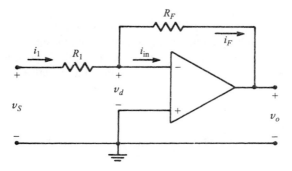

Fig. 8-2 Inverting amplifier

Example 8.2 For the inverting amplifier of Fig. 8-2, find the voltage gain v_o/v_S using (a) only characteristic 1 and (b) only characteristic 2 of the ideal op amp.

Solution: (a) By the method of node voltages at the inverting input, the current balance is

$$\frac{v_S - v_d}{R_1} + \frac{v_o - v_d}{R_F} = i_{in} = \frac{v_d}{R_d} \tag{8.2}$$

where R_d is the differential input resistance. By (8.1), $v_d = v_o/A_{OL}$ which, when substituted into (8.2) gives

$$\frac{v_S - v_o/A_{OL}}{R_1} + \frac{v_o - v_o/A_{OL}}{R_F} = i_{in} = \frac{v_o/R_d}{A_{OL}} \tag{8.3}$$

In the limit as $A_{OL} \to \infty$, (8.3) becomes

$$\frac{v_S}{R_1} + \frac{v_o}{R_F} = 0 \qquad \text{so that} \qquad A_v = \frac{v_o}{v_S} = -\frac{R_F}{R_1} \tag{8.4}$$

(b) If $i_{in} = 0$, then $v_d = i_{in} R_d = 0$ and $i_1 = i_F = i$. The input and feedback-loop equations are, respectively,

$$v_S = iR_1 \qquad \text{and} \qquad v_o = -iR_F$$

whence

$$A_v = \frac{v_o}{v_S} = -\frac{R_F}{R_1}$$

in agreement with (8.4).

The *noninverting amplifier* of Fig. 8-3 is realized by grounding R_1 of Fig. 8-2 and applying the input signal at the noninverting op amp terminal. When v_2 is positive, v_o is positive and current i is positive. Voltage $v_1 = iR_1$ then is applied to the inverting terminal as negative voltage feedback.

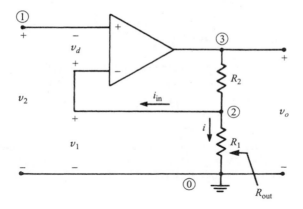

Fig. 8-3 Noninverting amplifier

Example 8.3 For the noninverting amplifier of Fig. 8-3, assume that the current into the inverting terminal of the op amp is zero, so that $v_d \approx 0$ and $v_1 \approx v_2$. Derive an expression for the voltage gain v_o/v_2.

Solution: With zero input current to the basic op amp, the currents through R_2 and R_1 must be identical. Thus

$$\frac{v_o - v_1}{R_2} = \frac{v_1}{R_1} \quad \text{and} \quad A_v \equiv \frac{v_o}{v_2} \approx \frac{v_o}{v_1} = 1 + \frac{R_2}{R_1}$$

The *common-mode gain* is defined (see Fig. 8-1) as

$$A_{cm} \equiv -\frac{v_o}{v_2} \tag{8.5}$$

where $v_1 = v_2$ by explicit connection. Usually, A_{cm} is much less than unity ($A_{cm} = -0.01$ being typical). Common-mode gain sensitivity is frequently quantized via the *common-mode rejection ratio* (CMRR), defined as

$$\text{CMRR} = \frac{A_{OL}}{A_{cm}}$$

and is expressed in decibels as

$$\text{CMRR}_{db} = 20 \log \frac{A_{OL}}{A_{cm}} = 20 \log \text{CMRR}$$

Typical values for the CMRR range from 100 to 10,000, with corresponding CMRR_{db} values from 40 to 80 dB.

Example 8.4 Find the voltage-gain ratio of the noninverting amplifier of Fig. 8-3 in terms of its CMRR. Assume $v_1 = v_2$ insofar as the common-mode gain is concerned.

Solution: The amplifier output voltage is the sum of two components. The first results from amplification of the difference voltage v_d as given by (8.1). The second, defined by (8.5) is a direct consequence of the common-mode gain. The total output voltage is then,

$$v_o = A_{OL}v_d - A_{cm}v_2 \qquad (8.6)$$

Voltage division (with $i_{in} = 0$) gives

$$v_d = v_1 - v_2 = \frac{R_1}{R_1 + R_2}v_o - v_2 \qquad (8.7)$$

and substituting (8.7) into (8.6) and rearranging gives

$$v_o\left(1 - \frac{A_{OL}R_1}{R_1 + R_2}\right) = -(A_{OL} + A_{cm})v_2$$

Then

$$A_v = \frac{v_o}{v_2} = \frac{-(A_{OL} + A_{cm})}{1 - A_{OL}R_1/(R_1 + R_2)}$$
$$= \frac{-A_{OL}}{1 - A_{OL}R_1/(R_1 + R_2)} - \frac{A_{OL}/\text{CMRR}}{1 - A_{OL}R_1/(R_1 + R_2)}$$

The *summer amplifier* (or *inverter adder*) of Fig. 8-4 is formed by adding parallel inputs to the inverting amplifier of Fig. 8-2. Its output is a weighted sum of the inputs, but inverted in polarity. In an ideal op amp, there is no limit to the number of inputs. However, the gain is reduced as inputs are added to a practical op amp.

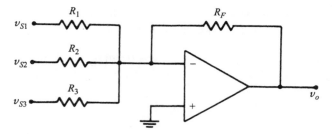

Fig. 8-4 Inverting summer amplifier

Example 8.5 Find an expression for the output of the inverting summer amplifier of Fig. 8-4 assuming the basic op amp is ideal.

Solution: We use the principle of superposition. With $v_{S2} = v_{S3} = 0$, the current in R_1 is not affected by the presence of R_2 and R_3 since the inverting node is a virtual ground. Hence, the output voltage due to v_{S1} is, by (8.4), $v_{o1} = -(R_F/R_1)v_{S1}$. Similarly, $v_{o2} = -(R_F/R_2)v_{S2}$ and $v_{o3} = -(R_F/R_3)v_{S3}$. Then, by superposition,

$$v_o = v_{o1} + v_{o2} + v_{o3} = -R_F\left(\frac{v_{S1}}{R_1} + \frac{v_{S2}}{R_2} + \frac{v_{S3}}{R_3}\right)$$

The introduction of a capacitor into the input path of an op amp leads to time differentiation of the input signal. The circuit of Fig. 8-5 represents the simplest *inverting differentiator* involving an op amp. As such, the circuit finds limited practical use, since high-frequency noise can produce a derivative whose magnitude is comparable to that of the signal. In practice, high-pass filtering is utilized to reduce the effects of noise.

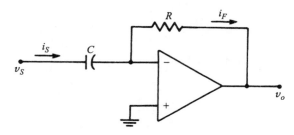

Fig. 8-5 Differentiating amplifier

Example 8.6 Find an expression for the output of the inverting differentiator of Fig. 8-5, assuming the basic op amp is ideal.

Solution: Since the op amp is ideal, $v_d = 0$ and the inverting terminal is a virtual ground. Consequently, v_s appears across capacitor C:

$$i_S = C\frac{dv_S}{dt}$$

But the capacitor current is also the current through R (since $i_{in} = 0$). Hence,

$$v_o = -i_F R = -RC\frac{dv_S}{dt}$$

The insertion of a capacitor in the feedback path of an op amp results in an output signal that is a time integral of the input signal. A circuit arrangement for a simple *inverting integrator* is given in Fig. 8-6.

Example 8.7 Show that the output of the inverting integrator of Fig. 8-6 is proportional to the time integral of the input signal, assuming the op amp is ideal.

Solution: If the op amp is ideal, the inverting terminal is a virtual ground, and v_S appears across R. Thus, $i_S = v_S/R$. But, with negligible current into the op amp, the current through R must also flow through C. Then,

$$v_o = -\frac{1}{C}\int i_F\, dt = -\frac{1}{C}\int i_S\, dt = -\frac{1}{RC}\int v_S\, dt$$

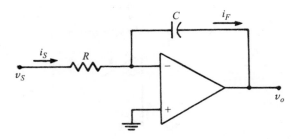

Fig. 8-6 Integrating amplifier

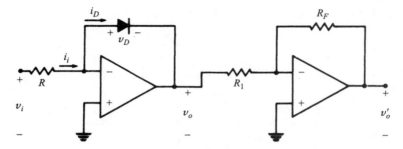

Fig. 8-7 Logarithmic amplifier

Analog multiplication can be carried out with a basic circuit like that of Fig. 8-7. Essential to the operation of the logarithmic amplifier is the use of a feedback-loop device that has an exponential terminal characteristic curve. One such device is the semiconductor diode of Chapter 2, which is characterized by

$$i_D = I_o(e^{v_D/\eta V_T} - 1) \approx I_o e^{v_D/\eta V_T} \tag{8.8}$$

A grounded-base BJT can also be utilized since its emitter current and base-to-emitter voltage are related by

$$i_E = I_S e^{v_{BE}/V_T}$$

Example 8.8 Determine the condition under which the output voltage v_o is proportional to the logarithm of the input voltage v_i in the circuit of Fig. 8-7.

Solution: Since the op amp draws negligible current,

$$i_i = \frac{v_i}{R} = i_D \tag{8.9}$$

Since $v_D = -v_o$, substitution of (8.9) into (8.8) yields

$$v_i = RI_o e^{-v_o/V_T} \tag{8.10}$$

Taking the logarithm of both sides of (8.10) leads to

$$\ln v_i = \ln R I_o - \frac{v_o}{V_T} \tag{8.11}$$

Under the condition that $\ln R I_o$ is negligible (which can be accomplished by controlling R so that $R I_o \approx 1$), (8.11) gives $v_o \approx -V_T \ln v_i$.

The use of op amps in active RC filters has increased with the move to integrated circuits. Active filter realizations can eliminate the need for bulky inductors, which do not satisfactorily lend themselves to integrated circuitry. Further, active filters do not necessarily attenuate the signal over the pass band as do their passive-element counterparts. A simple *inverting, first-order, low-pass filter* using an op amp as the active device is shown in Fig. 8-8.

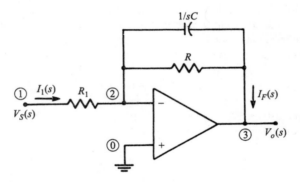

Fig. 8-8 First-order low-pass filter

Example 8.9 (*a*) For the low-pass filter whose s-domain (Laplace-transform) representation is given in Fig. 8-8, find the transfer function (voltage-gain ratio) $A_v(s) = V_o(s)/V_S(s)$. (*b*) Draw the Bode plot (M_{db} only) associated with the transfer function to show that the filter passes low-frequency signals and attenuates high-frequency signals.

Solution: (*a*) The feedback impedance $Z_F(s)$ and the input impedance $Z_1(s)$ are

$$Z_F(s) = \frac{R(1/sC)}{R + 1/sC} = \frac{R}{sCR + 1} \qquad \text{and} \qquad Z_1(s) = R_1$$

The resistive circuit analysis of Example 8.2 extends directly to the s domain. Thus,

$$A_v(s) = -\frac{Z_F(s)}{Z_1(s)} = -\frac{R/R_1}{sRC+1} \tag{8.12}$$

(*b*) Letting $s = j\omega$ in (8.12) gives

$$M_{db} \equiv 20\log|A_v(j\omega)| = 20\log\frac{R}{R_1} - 20\log|j\omega RC + 1|$$

A plot of M_{db} is displayed in Fig. 8-9. The curve is essentially flat below $\omega = 0.1/RC$. Thus, all frequencies below $0.1/RC$ are passed with the dc gain R/R_1. A 3-dB reduction in gain is experienced at the corner frequency $1/\tau = 1/RC$ and the gain is attenuated by 20 dB/decade of frequency change for frequencies greater than $10/RC$.

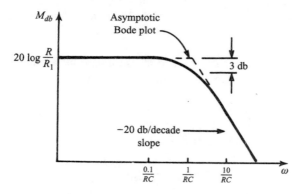

Fig. 8-9 Low-pass filter response

Frequently in analog system design, the need arises to modify amplifier gain in various ways, to compare signals with a generated reference, or to limit the signals depending on their values. Such circuit applications can often be implemented with high-input-impedance, low-output-impedance and high-gain characteristics of the op amp. The possibilities for op amp circuits are boundless. Typically, however, nonlinear elements (such as diodes or transistors) are introduced into negative feedback paths while linear elements are used in the input branches.

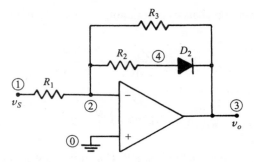

Fig. 8-10 Signal-conditioning amplifier

Example 8.10 The signal-conditioning amplifier of Fig. 8-10 changes gain depending upon the polarity of v_S. Find the circuit voltage gain for positive v_S and for negative v_S if diode D_2 is ideal.

Solution: If $v_S > 0$, then $v_o < 0$ and D_2 is forward-biased and appears as a short circuit. The equivalent feedback resistance is then

$$R_{Feq} = \frac{R_2 R_3}{R_2 + R_3}$$

and using the results of Example 8.2,

$$A_v = -\frac{R_{Feq}}{R_1} = -\frac{R_2 R_3}{R_1(R_2 + R_3)}$$

If $v_S < 0$, then $v_o > 0$ and D_2 is reverse-biased and appears as an open circuit. The equivalent feedback resistance is now $R_{Feq} = R_3$ and

$$A_v = -\frac{R_{Feq}}{R_1} = -\frac{R_3}{R_1}$$

Important Things to Remember

✔ Operational amplifiers consist of several semi-conductor devices integrated into a single amplifier circuit.

✔ In many circuit applications, the ideal model of the op amp can be used to simplify the analysis with negligible error.

✔ Many op amp circuits (filters, summing circuits . . .) use the straightforward analysis developed for the inverting amplifier.

✔ Analog mathematical functions (integrating, differentiating . . .) can be implemented with op amp circuits.

Additional Solved Problems

ASP 8.1 A *differential amplifier* (sometimes called a *subtractor*) responds to the difference between two input signals, removing any identical portions (often a bias or noise) in a process called *common-mode rejection*. Find an expression for v_o in Fig. 8-11 that shows this circuit to be a differential amplifier. Assume an ideal op amp.

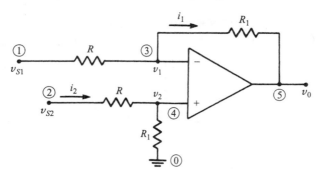

Fig. 8-11 Circuit for ASP 8.1

Solution: Since the current into the ideal op amp is zero, KVL gives

$$v_1 = v_{S1} - Ri_1 = v_{S1} - R\frac{v_{S1} - v_o}{R + R_1}$$

By voltage division at the noninverting node,

$$v_2 = \frac{R_1}{R + R_1}v_{S2}$$

In the ideal op amp, $v_d = 0$ so that $v_1 = v_2$, which leads to

$$v_o = \frac{R_1}{R}(v_{S2} - v_{S1})$$

Thus, the output voltage is directly proportional to the difference between the input voltages.

ASP 8.2 The circuit of Fig. 8-12 is an *adjustable-output voltage regulator*. Assume that the basic op amp is ideal. Regulation of the Zener is preserved if $i_Z \geq 0.1I_Z$ (see Chapter 2). (*a*) Find the regulated output v_o in terms of V_Z. (*b*) Given a specific Zener diode and the values of R_S and R_1, over what range of V_S would there be no loss of regulation?

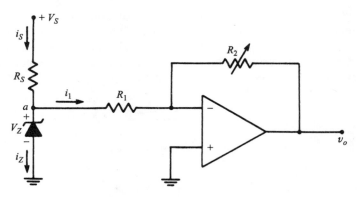

Fig. 8-12 Circuit for ASP 8.2

Solution: Since V_Z is the voltage at node a, (8.4) gives

$$v_o = -\frac{R_2}{R_1}V_Z$$

So long as $i_Z \geq 0.1I_Z$, a regulated value of v_o can be achieved by adjustment of R_2.

(*b*) Regulation is preserved and the diode current $i_Z = i_S - i_1$ does not exceed its rated value I_Z if

$$0.1I_Z \leq i_S - i_1 \leq I_Z \qquad \text{or} \qquad 0.1I_Z \leq \frac{V_S - V_Z}{R_S} - \frac{V_Z}{R_1} \leq I_Z$$

or

$$0.1I_Z R_S + \left(1 + \frac{R_S}{R_1}\right)V_Z \leq V_S \leq I_Z R_S + \left(1 + \frac{R_S}{R_1}\right)V_Z$$

Index